MENORCA

BY
LINDSAY BENNETT

Produced by
Thomas Cook Publishing

Written by Lindsay Bennett
Photography © Pete Bennett

Edited and designed by Laburnum Technologies Pvt Ltd,
C-533 Triveni Apts, Sheikh Sarai Phase 1,
New Delhi 110017

Published by Thomas Cook Publishing
A division of Thomas Cook Tour Operations Limited

PO Box 227, Unit 18, Coningsby Road,
Peterborough PE3 8SB, United Kingdom
E-mail: books@thomascook.com
www.thomascookpublishing.com
Tel: +44 (0) 1733 416477

ISBN 13: 978-1-84157-580-3
ISBN 10: 1-84157-580-1

Text © 2006 Thomas Cook Publishing
Maps © 2006 Thomas Cook Publishing

First edition © 2006 Thomas Cook Publishing

Project Editor: Linda Bass
Production / DTP Editor: Steven Collins

Printed and bound in Spain by: Grafo Industrias Graficas, Basauri

Cover design by: Liz Lyons Design, Oxford
All images front and back cover © Thomas Cook Publishing

Contents

KEY TO MAPS

✈	Airport	⬩	Viewpoint
Ⓟ	Parking	ME-1	Road No.
★	Start of walk /drive		
124.5m ▲	Mountain		
ⓘ	Information		
✝	Church		

Introduction

Sex and sun and rock and roll tend to be the first things people think about when you mention the Balearics. These pretty islands scattered in the western Mediterranean have gained a reputation as the destination where an entire generation of Northern European youth heads to pass a week or two in a haze of artificially induced pleasure while cultivating a deep tan to impress their mates back home.

Fun at the beach

But while this may be partly true of Ibiza and Mallorca, the two most visited islands, you'd be wrong to think so about Menorca. This is the island that paused to think when the tourist dollars began to roll in, turned its back on the raucous, booze-fuelled clubbing market and took a different direction.

Menorca has deliberately limited its tourist development. After a few early errors, the new development is tasteful and low-rise, in sympathy with the landscape and not working against it. It has marketed itself as 'the family island' but this certainly doesn't preclude the young, the single and those without kids. The warm and relaxed welcome and resort activities are low-key and it is a great place to get active on land or

water, on two legs or two wheels, on four legs (equine) or with a scuba tank strapped to your back.

The island's magnificent coastline is its most stunning asset. From cosy rocky inlets to vast stretches, the golden beaches are caressed by azure waters that make an excellent playground for yachtsmen – and their white-masted vessels anchored offshore only add to the picture-perfect vista. Where the sand stops the limestone begins, its surface eroded into surreal shapes and narrow valleys, and cut by numerous caverns.

Nature's raw material has been in good hands for centuries, sculpted by man since before the Bronze Age. History has cast a long and languorous shadow here, and you can spend more than a day or two clambering amongst dusty ancient stones or marching to the beat of the military drum of many a colonial army.

For generations the Menorcans have seen powerbrokers from the rest of Europe come and go while working the land and fishing the seas. Ties with the island's tradition are strong even in the face of 21st-century modernity and tourism seems to flow with this tradition rather than crowding it out.

UNESCO recognised the Menorcans' unique relationship with their land in 1994 when they awarded the island the coveted 'biosphere reserve' status. Plans are afoot to add over half the land mass to the protected list, further enhancing its 'green' credentials. This is going to be one of Europe's favourite all-round destinations over the next few years.

Mayonnaise: A Culinary Gift to the World

Menorca's most famous gift to the world was invented during the French suzerainty of the island. The official version that the sauce was invented by the French chef to the Duke de Richelieu is hotly disputed by the Menorcans who are pretty sure that this chef stole the recipe from a local girl working in the kitchen and called it his own – naming it Mayonnaise or Mahonnaise after the Menorcan capital Mahon, now Maó. Fast food wouldn't be the same without it!

A typical rural home in Menorca

The pretty white houses of Alaior

The Land

Menorca is a small island but its geological diversity is impressive. Its relative isolation has led to the preservation of a number of rare species and the development of several species found only here or on the sister Balearic Islands. Menorca can be divided in landscape and climate into north and south, named after the winds that play across the land – the migjorn of the south and the tramuntana of the north.

A Menorcan farm

The Migjorn (the South)

Menorca's south is the area that first welcomes the warm southerly winds from Africa. The limestone and sandstone substrate was laid down during the Miocene era; since then, it has been eroded by wind and water into hundreds of shallow steep valleys or barrancas ending in narrow inlets that house the island's famous cala resorts. The vegetation is much more lush here,

The coastline around Punta Prima

sheltered from the winds, with orange and holm oak groves.

The Tramuntana (the North)

The north offers a totally different landscape with deep inlets and dramatic rock formations. The northerly winds hold sway here and, particularly in winter, they race across the northern Mediterranean at up to 90kph hitting the lowlands of Menorca. Here you will find low-growing, 'alpine-type' scrubland and wild olives bent against the prevailing airflow. In some places there is no vegetation at all, and man-made structures like the ancient talayots or the more modern barraques (majestic stone sheep pens) stand sentinel against the skyline.

The Transition Zone

Where north meets south there is a fertile transition zone where much of the island's farmland can be found. The main cross-country route through the island, the ME-1, runs through the heart of this zone past fields replete with wild flowers in the spring, maize in summer, and ripening citrus and olives in the autumn.

Biosphere Reserve

Menorca joined over 410 locations worldwide when UNESCO declared the whole island a biosphere reserve in 1993 in recognition of the unique relationship between the islanders and the landscape. This acknowledges the efforts made by the local population to develop in a sustainable way with respect to the landscape and cultural traditions.

UNESCO define biosphere reserves as 'areas of terrestrial and coastal ecosystems promoting solutions to reconcile the conservation of biodiversity with its sustainable use'. Biosphere reserves serve in some way as living laboratories for testing out and demonstrating integrated management of land, water and biodiversity. Each biosphere reserve is intended to fulfil three basic functions, which are complementary and mutually reinforcing:

A conservation function – to contribute to the conservation of landscapes, ecosystems, species and genetic variation.

A development function – to foster economic and human development that is socio-culturally and ecologically sustainable.

A logistic function – to provide support for research, monitoring, education and information exchange related to local, national and global issues of conservation and development.

Regions of Menorca

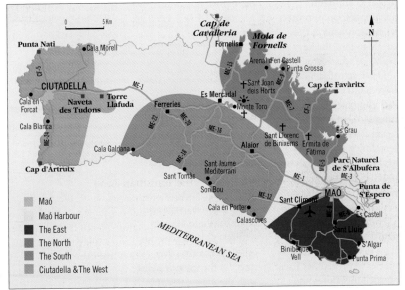

Maó
Maó Harbour
The East
The North
The South
Ciutadella & The West

Local Menorcans sit on the streetside watching tourists

(www.unesco.org/mab/nuts hell.htm)

Environment Protection

The Menorcan Council has prepared an Island Territorial Plan to protect its environment in the coming years, the key points of which are:

Limiting urban growth in certain key areas including controlling future tourist complexes.

Implementation of a recycling programme – not easy with such a small base population as recycling programmes are expensive per head.

Protection of natural native ecosystems by taking steps to eradicate foreign species of plants that have invaded the shores and taken over the native plants.

Funding research into the history and cultural heritage of the island.
For further details contact the Consell Insular de Menorca. Tel: 902 35 60 50. www.cime.es

Flora

Menorca has less diversity then the other Balearic Islands, perhaps because the strong winds stop the propagation of some delicate species. The uncultivated areas offer acres of hardy Mediterranean holm oak and wild olive or oleaster, often bent into bizarre shapes. Fragrant pines and other evergreens cover tracts of the interior along with the mastic tree that

THOMAS COOK TRAVELLERS MENORCA

We have divided this book into a number of discreet 'What to See' sections.

The capital Maó deserves its own chapter. Then we move on immediately to the attractions around the Maó inlet. Southeast Menorca is compact but packed with attractions and bursting with cultivated greenery. Then we move on to the wild natural beauty of the north. The south includes the main coastal resorts, but we have added the towns of the hinterland in this section, keeping all the communities strung along the main island road together. Finally, there is a section on the west, its main settlement, Ciutadella, and the resorts and attractions that surround it.

releases a useful resin. In the northern extremities the rocky headlands are blanketed in a low-growing 'socarrells' of wild herbs and sturdy species such as heather, lentisk and box, while each sheltered barranca in the south is its own unique ecosystem, the most complex hosting well over 100 different species. Along some of the more remote beaches it is possible to find wild lilies.

Fauna

Menorca is renowned for its bird-life (*see pp168–9*) with a year-round wealth of predator birds. The other highlight of its fauna are reptiles. The protected offshore islands are home to rare species found only here. The Balearic rabbit and the short-legged vole also make a rare appearance, as does the voracious pine marten.

The People

There are just over 70,000 Menorcans most of whom speak Menorquí, a dialect of Catalan. Three-quarters of the island's inhabitants live in the two major towns, Maó and Ciutadella. The Roman Catholic faith is a strong force that binds the community together, and tourism is the economic lifeblood that feeds the comparatively high per capita income of Menorcans when compared with other parts of Spain.

A geological divide

The bay of Cala Morell (*see p122*) sits astride a geological fault that slices through Menorca. This is most easily seen by the totally different colour and constitution of the rocks on the east and west sides of the bay. A flight of steps has been carved at the site of the fault at the eastern end of the bay.

The popular beach of Cala'n Porter

History

Despite its diminutive size, Menorca has had a long and sometimes tumultuous history, often as a pawn in the games of more powerful dynasties or countries. Though the island has also been a bit player in the history of Spain, the information here concentrates on the Menorcan perspective of the last 6,000 years.

Ram statue in old town Maó

c. 4000 BC	The earliest evidence of human settlement on the island but little is known about these people beyond the fact that they were farmers and hunters. Late in this period, caves are used for housing and as ritual sites.
c. 2500 BC	The first 'Megalithic' structures begin to be built.
c. 1400 BC	Evidence of cross-cultural and technological trade between ancient Menorcans and the Beaker people. The Talayotic era begins around this time.
Early 1st millennium BC	Trading contacts are made with the Phoenicians and Greeks.
c. 3rd century BC	Carthiginians take the island by force. Their main settlement on the site of today's Maó is called Magón (after Magó, brother of Hannibal), while a settlement on the site of present-day Ciutadella was named Jamma. Later, during the Punic Wars, the Balearic Islands are a valuable Carthiginian base for attacks further east to the heart of Rome; but, as Rome becomes more powerful, Carthage retreats to northern Africa.
123 BC	The Romans take the island, giving it the name Minorica.
1st century BC–3rd century AD	Stability under Rome, which introduces olive oil and grapes to the island. Port Magonum (Maó) is the administrative capital.
AD 404	The Balearics become a separate Roman province.
420s	Vandals arrive in the immediate aftermath of the fall of Rome and systematically destroy towns and churches.

533	Byzantine forces rout the Vandals and Menorca becomes part of the empire ruled from Constantinople, through feudal chieftains.
8th and 9th centuries	Raids by Muslim forces from the north coast of Africa. Byzantine control is loosened.
903	Menorca is taken by Muslim Moors under the control of the Emir of Cordoba.
1015	After the Cordoba regime collapses, the island comes under the influence of the Taifa Muslims at Denia.
1085	The Balearics become an independent Muslim 'emirate'; Christians begin to be persecuted, to the anger of surrounding Papist nations.
early 12th century	A Norman Christian invasion is repelled by the Muslims.
1116	The Almoravides Muslims take over, starting a period of relative calm.
1203	The Almohad Muslims take custody of the islands.
1229	Jaime I (ruler of Catalonia and Aragon) takes Mallorca by force and, in 1232, Menorca by negotiation. Ciutadella is reinforced as the leading town of the island.
1276	Death of Jaume. Menorca becomes part of the kingdom of Mallorca. The following few years see the island swing between Mallorca and Aragon.
1344	Pedro of Aragon retakes the island. Jaume III dies trying to recapture his kingdom in 1349.
1348	The Black Death hits the population.
early 15th century	The island is on the verge of civil war with the countryside in revolt against taxes.
1463	A civil war breaks out as the countryside supports Joan II. Ciutadella stays loyal to the King.
1469	The marriage of Isabella of Castile to Ferdinand of Aragon unites the Spanish under one 'crown'.
1535	The Ottomans arrive in the Balearics. Maó is sacked by Barbarossa and Castell Sant Felip is built

	to protect the harbour; many Menorcans are taken into slavery.
1558	Ciutadella falls into Turkish hands in what was to become 'the year of misfortune'.
1627	Ciutadella is forced to relinquish some of its administrative control to other towns on the island.
1706	The vacant throne of Spain results in the pan-European Spanish War of Succession. The island's population is split between the two opposing camps of Archduke Carlos and Philip. Philip takes the crown.
1708	The British take Menorca for the first time, ostensibly in support of Carlos but actually to gain control of another major Mediterranean port.
1713	The Treaty of Utrecht concludes the Spanish War of Succession. It also affirms Britain's territorial right to Menorca.
1722	Maó becomes the island's capital, and a British naval base.
1756	The French take Menorca during the Seven Years War. They build the town of Sant Lluís.
1763	The British return to Menorca.
1782	Charles III of Spain takes Menorca in a combined Franco-Spanish offensive. Castell Sant Felip is destroyed.
1798	The British return for the final time, taking control during the Napoleonic Wars.
1802	Menorca is formally given over to Spanish rule under the Treaty of Amiens. Castilian becomes Spain's official language and the Catalan spoken on the islands a secondary language.
1820	The Menorcan economy collapses due to a ban on movement of cereals. Mass migration to North Africa.
1830	After the French take Algiers, more Menorcans leave the island to set up home there.
1850	The first footwear factories are founded in Ciutadella.

1860	Isabel II, Queen of Spain, visits the new fortifications at La Mola – the fort is named in her honour.
late 19th and early 20th centuries	The footwear industry stalls as a major market, Cuba, becomes independent. Another wave of migration, this time to the USA, sees Menorca's population drop.
1936	The Spanish Civil War rents the country apart. Menorca remains loyal to the existing Republic but much bloodshed is prevented by a negotiated surrender.
1936–75	The Catalan language is repressed by Franco. Mainland Spaniards move to the island, mixing the population for the first time in many years.
1950s	The first seeds of mass tourism are sown.
1975	Death of Franco and reinstatement of the Spanish monarchy as part of a parliamentary democratic constitution.
1983	The Balearics (Formentera, Ibiza, Mallorca and Menorca) become a semi-autonomous region in a reorganisation of the Spanish system. The Menorcan Island Council is inaugurated, giving the population limited self-determination.
1986	Spain joins the precursor of today's EU, the European Community.
1993	Menorca is awarded the Biosphere Reserve title by UNESCO under its programme 'Man and Landscape'.
late 20th century	Catalan once again becomes the official language.
2002	A proposed tourist tax is shelved after complaints from tourism companies.
2004	Menorca remains staunchly Conservative as Socialists sweep to power in the wake of the Al Qaeda bombings in Madrid.
2005	The Council of the Balearics Islands announce a new daily tax on rental cars, to be commenced in 2006. The National government in Madrid slams the decision.

The House of Aragon

More complicated than the plot of any soap opera, the history of the house of Aragon includes more than a few murders, illegitimate births, family fall-outs and religious wars. Much of what we call Spain and southern France was the domain of three sovereign houses who married one another and fought one another for centuries to gain and keep territory and power.

The early Counts of Aragon started to build a power base in the opening decade of the 9th century but their antecedents and precise details are sketchy. It is thought that the dynasty began when Frankish nobles from France migrated to what is now northern Spain.

In 926 the family married into the house of Navarre and the Duchy continued until the reign of Sancho III or The Great when the dukes were transformed into kings – what historians now call the 'Kingdom of Aragon and Navarre'.

In the mid-12th century, Petronila of Aragon married the Count of Barcelona, Ramon Berengeur, creating the dynastic 'House of Barcelona'. During his reign (1213–76), James I conquered Ibiza and Mallorca (in c1228), and Valencia in 1238; his successor Peter III added Sicily. It was Alfonso III who brought Menorca into the fold. The Barcelona line died out with Martin I in 1410 and it was a couple of years before the Trastamara dynasty took the vacant throne.

The dynastic line was solidified in the person of Ferdinand II (1479–1516) whose reign was undisputed. He married Isabella of Castile and this act is considered by historians to have been a pivotal point in the history of

This dynastic alliance of Aragon and Castile thrust the family into the big time as the line quickly produced Charles I of Spain and Charles V Holy Roman Emperor (also of the House of Austria). Throughout the 1500s and 1600s, a series of Habsburg (Aragonese) rulers held sway over the area but in 1700 Charles II died without heirs. The power vacuum that followed resulted in the Spanish War of Succession. In 1714, the accession of Archduke Charles of Austria and the consolidation of power in the entity of Spain brought the Catalan–Aragonese confederation to an end.

greater Spain – the point when the houses stopped fighting with each other and started working on a wider consensus.

However, the marriage didn't result in a merger of these two royal 'corporations'; it was in many ways an accord rather than a contract, and the two monarchs had quite different priorities. For Ferdinand, the preservation of his Mediterranean kingdom including Menorca (but also Sicily and Sardinia) took precedence, while Isabella was keen to push the Moors from the Iberian peninsula and replace Islam with Christianity. She also funded a little trip by one Christopher Columbus that changed the course of history.

Facing page: King Alfonso III
Above: The Spanish coat of arms

HOW ARAGON WORKED

The Kingdom of Aragon on mainland Spain was never a true sovereignty. The territory consisted of a series of independent provinces each ruled by a 'Cortes' who worked in close consensus with the current ruler. This was much more a mercantile than a territorial or ideological empire, thriving in trade from port cities such as Barcelona. Unfortunately, as time went on they came under pressure from competitors, including the very successful Genoese, and friction in the eastern Mediterranean took up a lot of their attention.

Governance

Menorca is one of four populated Balearic Islands which are territorially part of the Spanish nation. The country has had a complicated political history and the present legislative organisation reflects these old territorial antecedents combined with the 'realpolitik' of the late 20th century. Today, Spain is the most devolved state in Europe with 17 autonomous regions and two autonomous cities. Menorca forms part of the Comunidad Autónoma de las Islas Baleares (Autonomous Region of the Balearics Islands), with a capital at Palma on the largest island, Mallorca. It has its own Consell Insular (Island Council).

A sign with a street named after King Alfonso III

Historical background

Strong regional identities have deep historic roots in the Spanish peninsula. In the beginning of the 16th century this country had been a mass of constantly fighting fiefdoms with each rising and falling in influence.

Even after Carlos I (better known as Charles V of Austria) was crowned King of Spain in 1516, some Spanish regions were still given specialist privileges, including Catalunya, and the seemingly unified monarchy was a mass of tensions between the various regional and bloodline factions. As late as 1931 when the government was overthrown and the Second Republic was declared, these were still in play. Catalunya declared itself independent and the Basques and Galicia were on the road to do the same when civil war broke out in 1936, the ensuing bloodbath resulted in the establishment of a military dictatorship headed by General Franco.

Franco suppressed any political debate, ruthlessly suppressing regionalism but when Spain entered a new era after his death in 1975 it was vitally important to manage these tensions to avoid the total melt down such as the one that followed Tito's death in Yugoslavia a couple of decades later. The politicians managed this pretty well by recognising and accommodating the differences. In the summer of 1977, a Minister for the Regions was appointed to assess the future. True federalism was ruled out, but during a two-year consultation period an agreement was reached between the various parties to form an autonomous assembly for regions whose populations demanded it.

Spain's prickly language issue was also tackled and the new constitution states that in addition to Castilian, Spain has three other official languages Basque, Catalan and Galician, though use of these languages is pretty much limited to their specific geographical regions.

Since Spain joined the pre-curser of the EU in 1986 this regional approach has been strengthened and supported by a pan European mandate to preserve minority languages and encourage and defend the cultural diversity in the lands within the Union.

The national institutions

Spain is a parliamentary democracy headed by King Juan Carlos I, who took the throne by popular mandate in November 1985. This position is hereditary but the role has no executive power, the monarch is essentially a national figurehead.

The legislative branch of government 'Las Cortes Generales' consists of two chambers. The first is the *senado* or senate consisting of 259 seats. Two hundred and eight of these are directly elected and 51 are appointed by the assemblies of the autonomous regions.

The Congress of Deputies is a 350-seat chamber whose members are appointed according to candidate lists under a proportional representation system. Each party is awarded a number of seats corresponding to their percentage of popular vote.

What's happening now

Spain's current government was elected in April 2004 and is led by the left wing Socialist Prime Minister José Luis Rodriguez Zapatero. However, the usually more conservative Menorcans stayed true to form and voted for the then incumbent centre-right government led by José Maria Aznar. The Menorcan Consell Insular (Island Council) has a conservative majority in the form of the Partido Popular.

The Autonomous Regions

The islands of the Balearics form one of the 17 autonomous regions of Spain. The rights of the autonomous regions are guaranteed by the constitution. The basic principle of autonomy is that the state recognises and guarantees the right of self-rule in the regions, provided they recognise the sovereignty of the greater Spanish nation.

The Menorcan and Spanish flags

The responsibilities of the governments of the various autonomous regions vary slightly but include the following:

Agriculture and Forestry
Commercial fishing
(within territorial waters)
Environmental protection
Health and hygiene
Housing
Local cultural affairs
Mineral and thermal waters
Museums and libraries
Non-commercial ports and airports
Public works
Preservation of monuments and historic buildings
Railways, canals and roads
Social assistance
Tourism
Town planning

The regional assemblies

The regional assemblies consist of a single chamber whose members or *diputados* are elected according to the national system of proportional representation. This system guarantees that all the political demands in communities are represented in the assembly. The *diputados* usually hold office for a period of four years. *Diputados* cannot sit in the national assembly but they do elect the senators who represent the community in the national Senate. Laws passed by regional assemblies are called territorial laws and are equal to, or have priority over state laws in areas where the local legislature has jurisdiction.

The Regional President

The president is the highest representative as well as the symbolic head of the autonomous region and represents the state.

He or she is responsible for the execution of national policy at the regional level and for duties as decided by each individual region, so the job varies from region to region.

Regional executive

The president and a team of ministers form the regional executive. The ministers are chosen from the *diputados* of the assembly and are responsible to them for all duties and decisions.

The judiciary

Each autonomous region has a *Tribunal Superior de Justicia*, a judicial body that deals with disputes involving regional law. It is also the highest judicial court within the territory, however it does not supercede the Supreme Court of Justice in Madrid in any matter.

Local politics in action

In a radical and controversial decision in 2003 the autonomous region of the Balearics voted to introduce a tourist tax on each arriving passenger (around 4 euros per person) that would be funneled directly into environmentally friendly projects. The tax was unpopular with hoteliers and the big holiday companies and bookings for the summer of 2004 dropped by over 10%, though surveys did not find a correlation between the levy and the drop in demand. In 2004 the government announced that it was scrapping the tax and that instead a 'green' foundation would be set up to provide funds.

The Town Hall displays the Menorcan flag

Culture

Menorca has mostly been on the fringes of any empire it has been a part of, and its contribution to the arts have not been on a grand scale. Instead, it has concentrated on cultivating its own homegrown 'arts', usually folkloric celebrations enjoyed by the population at fiestas and other holidays. Today, however, there is a lively cultural life and the island has one or two surprises up its sleeve.

Tourists enjoy Ciutadella, a major cultural venue

Theatre and Opera

You will find a surprisingly varied classical arts programme, concentrated in the two main towns of Maó and Ciutadella.

The Teatre Principal in Maó, built at the end of the 18th century, is Spain's oldest opera house and the island's premier cultural venue (*Costa d'en Deià 40, Maó; tel: 971 35 56 03; www.teatremao.org*). It is home to the Fundació de Teatre Principal, an organisation that promotes the arts throughout Menorca and offers programmes of classical and modern performances in the elegant Neo-classical interior.

The Teatre des Born on Plaça d'es Born in Ciutadella is the major cultural venue in western Menorca (*Plaça d'es Born; Ciutadella town hall; tel: 971 38 10 50*). It hosts plays, opera and other live music throughout the year. On the outskirts of the city, the Caritas de s'Hostal (the old quarry) has been imaginatively turned into an open-air venue and is gaining a reputation for its great acoustics (*Camí Vell; tel: 971 48 15 78*).

What a Voice

The island's most famous living son is Joan Pons Álvarez, born in Ciutadella in 1946 and now one of the world's foremost operatic baritones. Pons made his debut at La Scala in 1980 and has performed at Covent Garden and the Metropolitan Opera House. He continues to perform occasionally on his

Teatre des Born, Ciutadella's main cultural venue

home island but tickets sell out instantly and you will be lucky to catch a performance.

Opera singer, Lluis Sintes, born in Maó, has followed in Pons' footsteps by performing internationally. Simon Orfila, another baritone, who was born on the island in 1976, completes the triumvirate.

Art

The island has a strong commitment to art, and several cultural centres host exhibitions by local and international artists. Two notable luminaries are Jose Torrent and Pere Daura I Garcia.

Jose Torrent

Jose Torrent was born in Ciutadella in 1904. Throughout his life he travelled the island painting the landscapes in strong vivid colours; he became known to the locals as the 'Menorcan Van Gogh'. Torrent died in 1990 and his old home in the town has been converted into a museum displaying over 100 original works that span his long career, plus many personal artefacts.
Museu Pintor-Torrent.
c/Sant Rafal.
Tel: 971 38 04 82.
Open: May–Oct Mon–Fri
11am–1pm & 7.30–9.30pm,
Sat–Sun 8–10pm. Admission free.

Pere Daura I Garcia

Born in Ciutadella while his family was on a trip away from their native Barcelona, Daura trained in Barcelona where he was taught by Picasso's father. In 1914 he ventured to Paris where he became entranced by Fauvism and exhibited with other Catalan artists.

In 1928 he married an American artist Louise Blair and while on their honeymoon they fell in love with a medieval mansion in St-Cirq Lapopie in France. In the late 1920s Daura toyed with Abstract art as a founder of the Cercle se Cercle group with close ties to

S'Hostal quarry is now an open-air concert venue

Kandinsky, Leger and Mondrian. He returned to Spain to fight for the Republicans in the Civil War but later, in 1943, settled permanently in the US, spending his summers in France. He died in 1976.

An exhibition of Garcia's paintings is on permanent display at the Diocese Museum in Ciutadella (*see pp127–8*).

Traditional Music and Dance

Traditional dance accompanied by traditional music has increased in popularity since the fall of the Franco regime, and many dance troupes across the island perform 'folkloric' displays.

Groups like the Arrels de Sant Joan from Ciutadella and Castell de Sant Filipe from Es Castell perform regularly around the island, usually at weekends. Every year the folk group Es Rebost organises the 'Ballades a sa Plaça', a programme of folkloric performances that are held at the Claustre del Carme in Maó (*Jun–Sept Thur 8.30 pm; admission free*). These offer the perfect opportunity to get to know traditional Menorcan music, dances (*see below*) and dresses, besides other Spanish dances like the *fandango, bolero* and *bullanguera*.

The *jota* is the most traditional of the Catalan dances, a performance by two people, accompanied in medieval times by a song, that was originally performed at wakes and funeral meetings to celebrate the dead but now is a part of every folkloric display. The Jota de Aragon is famous throughout Spain.

In the Balearics, the *jota* spawned the *mateixa*, again performed by only two dancers but after each set of movements

one of the dancers is replaced by a fresh performer so that it is almost like a dance 'round'.

The *copeo* has a faster tempo and is a group dance for several couples. Tradition links it to celebrations, performed when a pig was slaughtered and roasted.

Cossiers are thought to be the oldest dances of the Balearics, and may well be an archaic vestige of complex ceremonies used by an old cult in the worship of agricultural deities because they are related to planting and harvest times. The dancers are men (always six in number) dressed as women, and they wear skirts and wide-brimmed hats decorated with flowers, ribbons and bells. They carry branches of basil and a handkerchief. With them is saintly 'Dama de Cossiers' (Lady of the Cossiers) and a devil, representing a confrontation between good and evil.

Musical Instruments

Menorcan dances have simple traditional musical accompaniment – the *flabiol*, a small wooden flute with five finger-holes played with the left hand, and the *tamborí*, a small side drum played with the right hand. The guitar came later in the island's history but is now an integral element of the greater 'Spanish' folkloric experience.

A British Touch

Es Castell (the old British Georgetown) still takes pride in its Scottish dances, where the performers wear kilts like the old Scottish regimental soldiers who used to be based here. However, the dancers perform to the sounds of the very Balearic *flabiol* and *tamborí*.

Neo-classical carving on Saura Palace

Architectural Styles

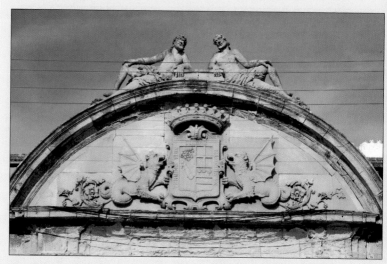

The colonial stewardship of Menorca over the years brought many architectural styles to the island. Here is a quick guide to post-ancient Roman architectural styles found here.

Early Christian/Byzantine

Named after Byzantium (or Constantinople), the capital of the Christian world in the late first millennium, this religious style was erected on a rectangular ground plan with a simple open structure and an entrance from the west. The floor plans can be seen at the basilicas at des Fornàs de Torelló (see pp68–9) and Son Bou (see p114).

Moorish

The Moors introduced the narrow arch into architecture; later, the style became recognisable by its pointed peak. Although many buildings were erected during their custody of Menorca, because of the animosity felt by the local people towards the Moors, the only Islamic architectural element left on the island is the tower of the Ciutadella cathedral.

Romanesque

This 11th and 12th century European style did not reach Menorca which was then under the influence of the Islamic Moors (see above).

Gothic

The Gothic style was a development of the Romanesque and its main feature is the pointed arch, which became extremely fine as the style developed. In churches and cathedrals, the western façade was the most impressive exterior feature, and these became more and more ornate over time. The south portal of the cathedral at Ciutadella is typical of the style.

Renaissance

The Renaissance or 'rebirth' revolutionised the arts in the 14th–16th centuries. The architectural style harked back to the Roman classics including the four styles of columns and the arch. However, Menorca has few fine Renaissance buildings as many were destroyed in the later Ottoman raids. Seek out Ermita de Sant Llorenc south of Arenal d'en Castell (see p85).

Baroque

The Baroque style was fashionable from the late 16th to mid-18th century, and is characterised by ornate decoration with the aid of columns, domes, pilasters and entablature. In Spain, a highly ornate form of Baroque called Churrigueresque, after architect José Benito de Churriguera, became popular. This Churrigueresque style can be viewed on the façade of the Església del Roser (see pp127) in Ciutadella.

Neo-classical

A backlash against Baroque in the late 18th century brought the purer lines now called the Neo-classical style. Its main characteristics are clean and uncluttered lines based on the mathematical formulas used by the ancient Greeks.

The British military and naval complexes at Es Castell (see pp52–4) and at the Arsenal (see p62) are good examples.

Art Nouveau and Art Deco

The two movements that kick-started the 20th century often used glass and iron in their designs. Art Nouveau was characterised by curved lines, while Art Deco moved on to a modern interpretation of classical straight lines. Casa Mir (pp45–6) and the Fish Market (see p44 & p48), both in Maó, are two contrasting early 20th-century buildings.

Domestic architecture

Llocs are traditional Menorcan farm complexes. These buildings are erected around a courtyard with a south-facing house and porxada – a large vaulted porch where the family live for much of the summer. There are barns and stables on the north side to protect the house against the prevailing tramuntana wind.

Facing page: A Neo-classical façade
Left: A Neo-classical bust

Musicians at a festival

Festivals and Events

You will find a packed programme of cultural events throughout the year in Menorca. Religious festivals are favoured, with Christmas, Carnival, Easter and Assumption Day being the most important. Parades are held across the island on these occasions with Easter being the time for more reverent processions. Sacred statues or paintings are solemnly paraded through the streets before the party begins.

In addition to this, every settlement has a festa (Castilian – fiesta) or feast day, celebrating the local patron saint. Further gatherings take place around harvest time when nature's bounty is celebrated. Menorca also holds several sporting events, though none that breaks on to the international stage.

Most Menorcan celebrations involve music

The following list only scratches the surface of events, so consult the tourist office to find out about what is happening during your stay on the island.

January
Diada de Sant Antoni (St Anthony's Day), honours the patron saint of Menorca. Ciutadella also celebrates the retaking of the island by Alphonse III in 1287 on this day. (**17 January**)

May
Verge del Torro
Festival of the Verge del Torro with a mass on Monte Toro and festivities in Es Merdacal. (**8 May**)
Menorca International Jazz Festival
There are performances throughout the month and all around the island during the Menorca International Jazz Festival.

June
Festa de Sant Joan (St John), the folkloric highlight of the year (*see p127 & p133*). (**23–24 June**)
The **Menorcan-Sant Joan Sailing**

Regatta is played out in the port of Maó. (**Late June**)

July

Ciutadella remembers the fateful attack of the Turks in 1558 which started the 'year of disgrace'. (**9 July**)

St Marti celebrations at Es Mercadal; Ciutadella holds the marine parade of **Verge del Carme. (mid-month)**

Procession of the Virgin of Carme in the port at Maó. (**16 July**)

Es Castell celebrates the **festival of Sant Jaume (St James). (24–26 July)**

Sant Antoni (St Anthony) celebrations at Fornells. (**4th weekend**)

Festival of St Peter in the port at Maó. (**29 July**)

Sant Cristòfol (St Christopher) celebrations in Es Migjorn Gran. (**last weekend**)

The **Festival de Musica d'Estiu** classical concert season in Ciutadella. (**through July & August**)

The **Maó International Music Festival** with classical concerts at Santa Maria Church and occasionally other venues. (**through mid-July–mid-September**)

'**Primavera Cultural**' and '**Estiu à Ferreries**' folkloric music and dance presentations at Ferreries. (**through July–September**)

August

Festival of Sant Llorenç (St Lawrence) with jousting in Alaior. (**first weekend after the 10th**)

Il Copa de Rey de Barcos de Epoca, a boat regatta with craft either vintage (pre-1949) or classic (1950–75), racing off Maó and mooring at the port by night. (**late in the month**)

Festival of Sant Climent (St Clement) in the town of the same name. (**20–22 August**)

Festival of Sant Bartomeu (St Bartholomew) at Ferreries. (**24–26 August**)

The '**King's Cup**' for period boats, and **festival of Sant Lluis** at Sant Lluis. (**last weekend August**)

September

Verge de Gràcia celebrations at Maó. (**7–8 September**)

Festival of St Nicholas at the summit of Monte Toro. (**10 September**)

October

Fun half-marathon around the streets of Ciutadella. (**1 October**)

'**Vuelta Cicloturistica**' amateur cycling tour of the island. (**third/ fourth week**)

Sant Antoni celebrations are held in Fornells every year

First Steps

Sitting in the Mediterranean Sea just east of Spain, Menorca is one of eleven islands and islets that make up the Balearics Islands – the easternmost one. Apart from Menorca, only three other islands are populated – Mallorca, Ibiza and Formentera, and each one offers a different landscape and character. As compared to the 'party' islands of Ibiza and Mallorca, Menorca may be considered the island for family fun and the 'great outdoors'.

The Town Hall façade, Maó

When to Go
Summer
Glorious blue skies, daytime temperatures in the late 20s°C, several hours of sunshine and long warm evenings draw thousands of visitors in the summer. Menorca is the epitome of the Mediterranean holiday destination in this season with the beaches coming into their own offering excellent swimming, snorkelling and diving opportunities and great boat trips if you don't want to get wet.

Of course the downside of the peak season (*late Jun–mid Sept*) is the sheer numbers of visitors putting pressure on the infrastructure. Roads, restaurants, marinas and hotels are chock-a-block; and it may be a little too hot for any strenuous activity like hiking and cycling.

Autumn
The crowds depart by the end of September, and churches and museums, plus the narrow alleys of Maó and Ciutadella become easier to explore. You will be able to find seats in the fashionable cafés once again and the roads are less congested. Temperatures are moderate in this season and, great for outdoor sports and activities; and the sun's warm glow is better for photographers than the harsh high summer light. For bird-spotters autumn is when the migratory birds stop off on their long journey south, making it an ideal time to visit.

The downside of a late visit is that the weather becomes less dependable with more chances of cloud cover and the odd spectacular thunderstorm. The evenings are cooler, so alfresco dinners might be off the menu.

Winter
By now the tourist crowds have long departed and many resorts seem to be completely closed; however, the winter season does have its compensations. Temperatures are warmer than in northern Europe, offering good conditions for hiking and cycling. You will also find a truly Catalan atmosphere around the island with the locals getting

on with life. Just watch out for the biting tramuntana, the wind that really chills the air.

Spring

Temperatures start rising again, as do the hours of sunlight. The birds return – heading north this time, and leaves on trees and budding crops look ahead to another fertile year. The canopies and umbrellas of the phalanx of waterside cafés and restaurants open like flowers, signalling that it's time for business. The tramuntana warms a touch but can still inflict a nasty sting when the temperature occasionally drops.

Just a thought!

It is worth noting that the cheap and regular charter packages and flights from the UK (and other parts of northern Europe) run from early May to the end of October. Many hotels are closed out of this 'season', making accommodation more difficult to come by.

What to wear

Layering is the byword here. In summer light cotton or breathable clothing is advisable for sightseeing. Take a long-sleeved item just in case your arms and shoulders get sunburnt but the weather

A tourist trying to find her way around!

A postcard rack

those who worship here and you'll be disrespectful if you visit scantily dressed.

What to See and Do

Without a doubt, the beaches are the primary draw of the island. The main resorts all have beautiful stretches and though most get crowded in August, it is easy to head out along the coast and find an equally if not more beautiful and less populated stretch of sand where you can lay out your towel and bronze to your heart's content.

Menorca is rich in prehistoric history and you may want to visit at least one of the dozens of Talayotic sites scattered across the land. If your interest is whetted you could fill a week or two and visit them all.

The two major settlements, Maó and Ciutadella – called cities though in size little more than large towns, are unmissable for their architecture and atmosphere. Both have picturesque ports with a jaunty nautical air, and great bars and shops.

Between days of sightseeing you can take to the water to windsurf or kayak or sail, head under the water with snorkel or scuba, or get out on the country lanes on foot or bicycle.

Menorca has some excellent and inexpensive restaurants where you can relax in the evenings over a long, satisfying meal.

Getting around

The bus services in Menorca are excellent for touring the main towns, with several Maó-to-Ciutadella connections every day travelling through Alaior, Es Mercadal and Ferreries. There

is reliable, so you shouldn't need any warm clothing. Swimsuits are not suitable attire for the towns and should be confined to the beaches – where topless bathing is perfectly acceptable.

Spring and autumn are warm, so carry light cotton outfits, but also pack a couple of warm layers (a fleece is ideal) especially for the evenings. The island can witness spectacular storms so a weatherproof jacket might be useful.

In the winter months, warm and waterproof clothing is advisable, though it certainly isn't unusual to be able to wear T-shirts in December or January. The evenings, however, will be chilly.

Whatever time of year you visit, it is wise to carry with you items of clothing that will cover the thighs and shoulders if you intend to visit churches and *ermitas*. These are spiritual places to

are also direct bus services to the capital from Punta Prima and the resorts of the southeast, and also from Maó to Es Grau and Fornells. Ciutadella is well linked to its surrounding resorts with regular services to Cala en Forcat and Cala'n Bosc. In the major resorts you will also find private companies who offer day tours by bus to the main attractions, often with a guide and lunch included.

However, to explore the remote beaches and the dozens of ancient sites dotted around the island, you will really need to rent a car even if only for a couple of days. A rental car puts you in charge of your own timetable and this is a relatively easy place to drive in with narrow lanes keeping speeds down, and no dual carriageways or fast roads to worry about. Menorcans are used to thousands of rental cars on their roads every summer, and are generally patient and courteous towards visitors.

Culture Shock

You are bound to find a few unusual and noteworthy differences between your homeland and Menorca. The following thoughts are a truly non-scientific approach to the idiosyncrasies of the island. They are in no particular order but simply offer a flavour of the national mind-set.

Tourists take a break at an outdoor café

Catalan v Castilian

Since Catalan has replaced Castilian as the official language of the island, you will notice names being changed and street signs duplicated so that Castilian Mahon becomes Catalan Maó, Alayor becomes Alaior and so on. Some of these changes take time, so don't be surprised to find different spellings for town and street names on maps and other tourist literature. In this book we have used the most common Catalan spellings unless the Castilian name is still used.

Siesta time

One factor that you must take into account when planning your sightseeing is siesta time. Because it is so hot in the summer it has become the tradition for

A group of young Menorcans

A shrine

everything to close in the afternoon when everyone rests or has a short nap, and for shops, museums, etc., to reopen as the air cools. Siesta time is usually from around 1pm until 4pm or 5pm. You will find that the major settlements turn into ghost towns between these hours. However, you won't find the same in the holiday resorts where shops remain open throughout the day.

How late?

Menorcans are fresh and raring to go in the evenings. They rarely eat before 9pm and often wait until later at weekends or on holidays. Children are still playing happily as midnight approaches and the streets are buzzing into the early hours of the morning, though there is never evidence of the drunken raucous behaviour found after a night out in northern Europe.

The paseo

The evening stroll is a Spanish institution. This is the time when neighbours chat, recent parents parade their babies, grandparents bill and coo, and courting couples only have eyes for each other. Weekend evenings see everyone dressed in their finest clothes.

Navigating

You can't really get lost in Menorca because you hit the coast or the main cross-island route sooner or later, but navigating does present a few problems primarily because there are few numbered lanes once you leave the main routes. Locals navigate not by road numbers but by the names of farms or hamlets.

Little touches of Blighty!

Look out for the small things, like push down door catches and sash windows in the mansions around Maó – and Premiership soccer on the big screens of Cala'n Porter and Cala en Forcat!

Ice cream

An ice cream is compulsory during the evening *paseo* and not just for children. Delicious sorbets and delicate fruit flavours entice adults too!

It is hard to resist the delicious treats at the ice-cream shops

PEIX i MARISC DE TERRA

català	castellà
ANFÓS	mero
BESUC	besugo
CABRA / CRANCA	centollo
CALAMAR	calamar
CALAMARSET	chipión
CONGRE	congrio
DÉNTOL	dentón
DONZELLA	doncella
ESCÓRPORA	escorpena
ESPARRALL	esparrayón
GALL	gallo
GERRET	caramel
LLAGOSTA	langosta
LLAGOSTÍ	langostino
LLAMPUGA	lampuga
LLENGUADO	lenguado
LLOBARRO	lubina
LLOMANTO / LLAMÁNTOL	bogavante
MANTA	rayón
MOLL	salmonete
MUSSOLA	mustelo / cazón
ORADA / DAURADA	dorada
PAGELL	besuguete
PEDAÇ	platija
PEIXET	pescadito
PEIXETÓ / MORALLA	moralla
PINXA / ARENGADA	arenque
POP	pulpo
RAJADA	raya
RAP	rape
ROJA / ROTJA / CAP-ROIG	raño
SARDINA	sardina
SARG / SARD	sargo
SERRA	serrano / cabra
SÍPIA / SÉPIA	sepia
SORELL	jurel
TURBOT	rodaballo
VACA	vaca / torpedo

To new arrivals in Menorca the Catalan v Castilian debate can seem confusing and in some ways irrelevant, but this issue cuts to the very heart of the Menorcan identity.

Both languages are classed as Iberian Romance, also known as 'New Latin', and they travelled south in the wake of the Reconquista (the pushing back of Moorish control south through the Iberian peninsula).

At that time different feudal power bases controlled different geographical areas – the rulers of Castile in central Spain spoke Castilian and Catalan was spoken by the Aragonese in Catalunya in northeast Spain, which also held sway over the Balearics in the wake of the Moorish retreat in the 13th century.

These two powerful dynasties were in constant battle with each other in the intervening centuries but eventually, after many inter-dynastic marriages, they reached an accord with the marriage of Ferdinand of Aragon and Isabella of Castile in 1479. The Aragonese were preoccupied with their Italian and Mediterranean territories and Castilian became the majority language across mainland Spain, though Catalan was used within its traditional geographical boundaries. Castilian was spread across the New World with the establishment of the Spanish colonies and became the lead dialect as administration developed.

This may not have mattered much when most Menorcans did not have much to do with life in Madrid or even on the mainland, but when Franco won the Civil War in 1936 he had a clear vision of what he wanted his Spain to be. In addition to ruthlessly stamping

* NAVEGUI PÓC A POC PER DINS DE LA CALA

* NAVEGA DESPACIO POR LA CALA

out any political opposition or dissent, he sought to quash many of the regional peculiarities of what was still a very diverse society, including the Catalan language.

Catalan printing presses were destroyed and newspapers closed down, and the teaching of the language in schools was banned. Though many Menorcans continued to learn to speak Calatan at home fewer learned to write it, and it wasn't until after Franco's death in 1975 that things started to change. After Spain joined the precursor of the EU in 1986, Catalan rose like a phoenix from the ashes of the dictatorship, nurtured by the European pledge to preserve regional or minority languages.

Today, Catalan is the official language of Catalunya, Valencia and the Balearics, and it is the primary language in schools and for all official institutions on Menorca. There are several daily newspapers printed in Catalan including the *El Dia del Mundo de Baleares* and *Ultima Hora*; Televisio Catalunya broadcasts across the region in Catalan and there is a 24-hour news channel.

Franco's legacy is that most Menorcans of native stock (as opposed to recent arrivals from mainland Spain) now speak both Catalan and Castilian, and you will have no trouble making

yourself understood in Castilian, nor will you come across any animosity if you communicate in Castilian. However, if you learn a few phrases in Catalan the already warm welcome will be just a little warmer and the wide smile just a little wider.

QUICK FACTS

Catalan: spoken by 7.5 million people in Andorra, Catalunya, Murcia, Valencia and the Balearic Islands in Spain; Rousillon in France, Alghero on Sardinia. Understood by a total of 12 million people.

Castilian: spoken by 330 million people in Spain, South and Central America with large populations in the United States of America. Understood by 417 million people.

Most signboards are dual-language, with instructions in Catalan and Castilian

Maó

Capital of the island since the 18th century, Maó can be about as bustling as Menorca gets but it is also a very approachable and relaxed city where you never feel overwhelmed by urbanism.

An Art Deco façade

Most visitors now arrive overland from the tourist resorts in the west of the island through the jumble of modern suburbs, but that was never the city's raison d'être. It thrived on its relationship with the water and its sheltered position close to the head of the inlet, and you get the best feel of the old heartbeat by starting your tour at the port. From the waterside the buildings of the old town seem to grow out of the living rock presenting a sheer face of sandstone and stucco hanging above the port and harbour below.

Cala de San Esteve

Once atop the cliffs you will find a compact old town of fine 18th- and 19th-century mansions held together by a web of narrow lanes and alleyways interspersed with tiny communal squares. Grand entranceways lead into three-storeyed homes whose windows are replete with fretted ironwork and shuttered windows, and the historical and religious attractions are firmly planted in the heart of this comfortable domesticity.

Maó only became capital of the island during the 18th century, and even then the religious hierarchy refused to decamp from their archdiocese at Ciutadella (*see pp124–35*). But the British went ahead and shifted the focus of the island to the east, away from siblings Mallorca and Ibiza. Today, however, though it was founded by the Royal Navy and you will still see a few small British touches, Maó is very much a Catalan Spanish town. There is a quiet confidence about the place since the demise of the Franco regime, the resurrection of the Catalan language and the decentralisation of power from Madrid to the Balearics.

The city certainly has enough attractions to fill a day. The Museum of Menorca is a must-visit attraction to help add a human story to the numerous ancient sites you will visit during your stay. But perhaps it is the atmosphere in the capital's streets that make it most worth a visit – especially in the early evenings when the entire population takes to the streets to stroll, socialise and romance. There is certainly a Latin magic about the place that lasts until the early hours of the morning.

Ajuntament (Town Hall)

The Town Hall was built in 1613 at the site of the city fortress but was given a smart new French Baroque overcoat in 1789 by architect Francisco Fernàndez de Angelo. The small clock was an afterthought added by Governor Kane (*see pp66–7*). It has a splendid façade replete with wrought-iron balconies and pompous pediments but it is difficult to admire the exterior because it sits at a rather unfortunate corner of Plaça de Constitució, plagued by passing cars and pedestrians. The building really deserves a better location.

The interior decoration is sumptuous, particularly the paintings and plasterwork in the Noble Hall and The Gallery of the Illustrious Menorcans. There is also a portrait of British King George III who ruled during much of his country's occupation of the island. *Plaça Constitució. Open: to the public daily 8am–2pm.*

Carrer Hannover

Part of the main shopping street that runs from Plaça de Constitució and Plaça de s'Esplanada, Carrer Hannover, is named after the Royal House of

Maó City

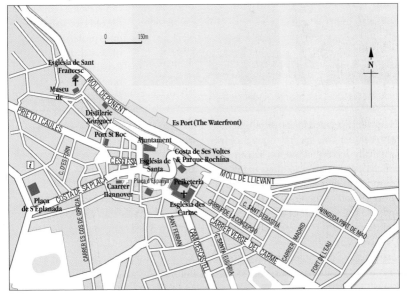

Costa de Ses Voltes was originally a ramp used for transporting cargo

Costa de Ses Voltes and Parque Rochina

This winding lane flanked by manicured parkland and a grand staircase for pedestrians was, until the mid-20th century, a wide ramp used to move cargo from the port. Today the road makes a good option for parking, and the gardens are a place for children to play, lovers to meet and old folks to sit and watch the world go by. It is interesting that these were an afterthought to the original grand design of the 1950s.

At either side of the base of the Costa you can view the remains of the old city walls that once protected Maó. The medieval and later Renaissance structures now form the foundations of more modern buildings that seem to grow out of the cliffs lining the port.

Hanover that ruled Great Britain in the 18th century (the spelling difference was originally accidental but has become official). Although Maó offers many examples of domestic architecture, this short section of the street is one of the most complete vistas in the city – an uninterrupted run of several buildings that form a coherent whole, and characterised by English details such as sash windows and bowed examples, known in Spanish as *boinders*.

Distilerie Xoriguer (Xoriguer Distillery)

The leading manufacturer of the distinctive Menorcan gin, Xoriguer is a family-owned company that launched the brand on the UK market in 2005. Xoriguer are still housed in one of the old warehouses down on the port side and you can see the distillery vats working their magic though you can't tour the works.

Xoriguer allow you to sample all their products before you buy and there is ample information in English about the ingredients in each though not the exact quantities, as the recipes are a guarded secret.

Distilerie Xoriguer. Andén de Poniente 91, 07701 Maó. Tel: 971 36 21 97. www.xoriguer.es. Open: Jun–Sept Mon–Fri 8am–7pm, Sat 9am–1pm; Oct–May Mon–Fri 9am–1pm & 4–7pm.

Església del Carme (Carmelite Church)

The Carmelite order gained permission from the British to build a church and convent, and the authorities approved this site, which stood outside the city walls at the time. The work was started in 1750; however, this coincided with a turbulent few decades in the island between the British, French and Spanish, and the complex was not completed until 1820. The huge façade almost imitates Port St Roc (*see p46 & p49*) with its two towers. It is devoid of embellishment save an extended arch around the doorway. This is the largest church in Maó but one of its least decorated.

The cloisters were almost immediately deconsecrated when the civil authorities grabbed church property across Spain, and they have been used for a number of civic purposes since 1835 including courtrooms and a prison. Today they serve as the city's fruit and vegetable market but also play host to Museu Hernández Mora (Hernandez Mora Museum). This museum is dedicated to the collections of one man, Joan Hernández Mora, who was a Victorian-era scientist, an art professor, archaeologist, archivist, artist and historian. His collection was donated to the city after his death in 1949 and comprises numerous works of art, furniture and household artefacts dating from the 18th to the 20th centuries, a cartography collection, and a library of works by Menorcan authors.

In front of the cloisters is a small patio where locals gather for a coffee in the Café Mirador. There are excellent views down to the harbour from here.

Museu Hernández Mora. Claustre del Carme 5. Tel: 971 35 05 97. Open: Mon–Sat 10am–1pm. Admission free.

Església del Carme entrance

A summer fair near St Mary's Church

Església de Sant Francesc (Church of St Francis)

Though the cloisters of the Franciscan monastery complex now house the Museum of Menorca (*see p42*), the adjoining church is still open for worship. Built on the foundations of an earlier Gothic church, the building of the present church was begun in 1719, and it was expanded throughout the century. The façade was not added until the 1800s.

The interior displays a single nave – as with the other major churches in the city. The major decorative elements, including paintings in the presbytery, are also 19th century. The mock-Baroque retablo (painting or framed image) above the main altar was added in 1945.

The Chapel of the Immaculate Conception is probably the finest entity within the church. Completed in 1752 the octagonal structure topped by an impressive cupola is linked to the main nave by a grand entrance portal. The decoration is extremely rich with a never-ending stream of carved vines and acanthus leaves in Churrigueresque style, attributed to artist Francesc Herrara.

Església de Santa Maria (St Mary's Church)

The first church of Santa Maria, patron saint of Maó, was erected by Alphonse III when he claimed the island in 1287. The church was totally rebuilt on the same ground plan in the 18th century in simple neo-Gothic style, so large that the interior is almost hangar-like. The main altar and side chapels however are Baroque – their high drama a contrast to the lines of the basic architecture.

The other major attraction of the interior is the vast organ built by the master organ builders Otter and Kirburz and the central feature at many of Maó's music festivals. Its shape echoes that of the altar with towering columns topped by triumphant statues, though the monotone gold/bronze colour lends an air of gravitas.

Open: daily 7.30am–1pm & 6–8.30pm. Organ recitals in summer daily between 11am & 11.30am.

Es Port (The Waterfront)

There is a lively atmosphere throughout the summer along the waterfront below the town. Once the heartbeat of the city, the economic impact of the port has diminished somewhat since the advent of tourism and the building of the airport, but commercial cargo and ferries from the mainland are still a regular feature. The yachting fraternity dock here for the restaurants and bars, and there is some great nightlife too.

Costa de Ses Voltes links the upper town at Place d'Espanya (*see pp44–6*) to the waterfront.

At the base of Ses Voltes you will find a gaily-coloured collection of boats offering trips around the harbour. Mediterranean cruise ships dock here – one of their most satisfying ports of call since you can step right out of the ship directly into the town. The main city

tourist office is also at the port, facing the main road.

To the west (left from the bottom of Ses Voltes) you will find the working heart of the port along Moll de Ponent: docks for cruise ships and, as you walk further towards the head of the inlet, ship repair yards and dry docks. You may want to make a trip to the Xoriguer Distillery (*see pp38–9*) housed in one of the old warehouses on the inland side of the port road.

To the east (right from the bottom of Ses Voltes) is a delightful route along the Moll de Llevant, the main pleasure dock of the city, where you will be accompanied by the sounds of hundreds

Es Port is a popular dock for yachtsmen

of halyards jangling in the breeze. On the quayside look out for the small bronze statue, *The Mô Mermaid* by Leonardo Lucarni, a symbol of the city and the port. There is a never-ending choice of café/bars and restaurants set under the crags where you can sit and watch the action, and in summer the fun goes on till dawn.

Museu de Menorca (Museum of Menorca)

Housed in a section of the monastery complex of St Francis of Assisi, the Museum of Menorca is the island's primary archaeological and historical collection, leading from the very awakening of the ancient lifestyles into the late second millennium.

The building itself demands some attention. Once through the ticket office

The Museum of Menorca

you will enter into a magnificent Baroque cloister that was completed just before the religious community was forced to leave in 1835, at the same time as the Carmelite community housed in the Carme complex (*see p39*). The fine stonework with its delicate and constrained embellishment, and the balanced form of the tiers of archways and windows offer a satisfying vista to the eye.

Temporary exhibitions are held on the ground floor of the building, while the museum occupies the upper two floors.

A short video that introduces the island offers some excellent landscapes in addition to extra information about where ancient finds were discovered. The galleries then move chronologically through time with good captions in English explaining what and where.

The first floor is devoted to the period from prehistory until the Byzantine era. Start with the pre-Talayotic finds of pre-1500 BC and then move into the Talayotic era proper where you will find artefacts of extreme sophistication – including the bronze statue of a bull found at the Torralba d'en Salord (*see p83 & pp116–17*) that has expanded the archaeologist's research into the religious beliefs of the Talayotic peoples. There are also interesting pieces relating to other cultures including a statue of Imhotep, the Egyptian High Priest c2600 BC and Punic pottery from mainland Italy. The Roman galleries include fascinating finds from a shipwreck discovered off the Cap de Favàritx.

On the second floor, the timeline starts with scant remains of the Moors and Aragonese. There are few artefacts from either time because the remaining population destroyed most Islamic buildings in the wake of their withdrawal and many Aragonese remains were lost in the Ottoman raids of the 1530s. The 17th and 18th centuries are much better represented through paintings, maps and everyday articles like English china or fine Catholic religious statuary rescued from churches across the island. As the Spanish finally took full control of the Balearics, industry arrived on the island, and the later galleries document this process. The final gallery displays paintings by Menorcan artists through the 20th century including the 'Group Menorca', a school dedicated to abstract expressionism.

Tiers of archways inside the Museum of Menorca

Maó's streets are packed with people in the early evening

The fish market is a wonderful example of modernist iron design

Next door to the museum is Església de Sant Francesc (*see p40 & p49*), the church of the original monastery complex.

Museu de Menorca. Avinguda Doctor Guàrdia s/n. Tel: 971 35 09 55. Open: Apr–Oct Tue–Sat 10am–2pm & 6–8.30pm, Sun 10am–2pm; Nov–Mar Mon–Fri 9.30am–2pm, Sat–Sun 10am–2pm. Admission charge.

Peixeteria (Fish Market)

Built on the foundations of an old bastion of the city wall in 1927 to a design by Francesc Femenías the municipal architect, the fish market is an excellent example of modernist iron and glass design that is well used to this day. You'll find fresh fish and shellfish of all kinds on ice here, plus live crabs and lobster – the perfect place to shop for dinner if you are self-catering.
Open: Mon–Sat 8am–1pm.

Plaça d'Espanya

For travellers arriving by boat, Plaça d'Espanya is the starting point for exploring the old town, and it is a rather confusing site. Designed in the 20th century during a major reconstruction of the city, it is classed as one of the major squares in the capital, yet it is not really a discernable square since it lies on a sloping piece of land and doesn't seem to have a defined shape. The fish market sits on the north flank, while the main section of the square that links it to Plaça de Carme and its vast church is cut by a couple of roads and a very difficult intersection leading down to

And so to market
Maó's main markets take place every Tuesday and Saturday mornings at the Plaça de s'Esplanada, a huge open space that was once a British parade ground for the regiment stationed in the capital.

the Costa de Ses Voltes (*see p48*) that is tricky for both drivers and pedestrians. On the plus side, the undulating skyline and the stucco façades add charm. The most impressive building in the square sits on the northwestern corner overlooking the port. Casa Mir with an elaborate glass façade, (not open to the public), was

Maó's Green Space

It would seem as you stroll around the city that there is little foliage to break up the rows of buildings and most of the city plaças are on the small side, but Maó does have some verdant greenery. Parc des Freginal is only a couple of minutes from the market place at Plaça de s'Esplanada or the central Plaça Constitució.

The Mô Mermaid sits on the quayside

A view of Maó and the harbour

built in the 1920s and is the finest 'modernist' building on Menorca.

Port St Roc

Incongruously surrounded by a close-order phalanx of narrow streets Port St Roc is the only vestige of the old medieval city wall and marked the city's boundary until the 18th century. The two strong towers rise above the rooftops, their slender arrow slits the main base for attack. The narrow entry portal now poses a problem for the two-way traffic that tries to muscle its way through, but when it was closed every night during medieval times the population would have slept soundly in

---

For more information
The Tourist office at Maó is situated at *Moll de Llevant 2 (on the waterfront at the bottom of the Carer de Ses Voltes).* *Tel: 971 35 59 52. www.e-menorca.org.*

---

their beds, secure within the walls. That was until 1535, when Barbarossa swept through the defences and ravaged the city. The gate, along with the rest of the walls, was badly damaged and had to be totally rebuilt.

Take a stroll

There are guided tours of Maó's old town (*summer Mon–Fri 7.30pm*). No need to book. The Town Hall is the starting point.

St Roc
St Roc was a 13th-century French nobleman who cared greatly for the suffering of the poor and the sick. On one of his pilgrimages he came upon a community suffering from the plague and stopped to tend the sick, eventually contracting the disease himself. He wandered into the forest expecting to die but was fed by a dog and recovered. In addition to being patron saint of plague sufferers, St Roc also helps people with knee problems and skin rashes.

Alphonso III
Though Jaume I took Menorca from the Moors for the house of Aràgon, he did not expel them from the island and left its administration in the hands of a Muslim *reis* or governor. It was not until 1287 that Islam was totally swept away, by Alphonso III, grandson of Jaume, and it is he who is remembered by the people as the saviour of the islands. There is a statue of Alphonso in Plaça de Constitució (on the north side of Església Santa Maria). It was presented to the island by General Franco in the 1950s.

Tourists take in the sites on Alphonso III street

The two towers of Port St Roc

Walk: A tour of Maó

Maó is easy to explore on foot. Everything is within easy reach and you should be able to sightsee without feeling jaded or 'over-museumed'.

Time: 3 hours.
Distance: 1.5km.

Start your trip from the tourist office on the quayside where you will be able to pick up maps and other information. Cross the road in front of the office and you will be presented with a rather daunting climb.

1 Costa de Ses Voltes

This is Costa de Ses Voltes, the grand entrance to the old town. This winding street cut with several flights of steps and finished with manicured greenery replaced the old cobbled ramp that the British had built to move cargo and men up into the town.

Climb the steps and when you reach the top (Plaça d'Espanya), turn left and cross the street (watch out for traffic as it could be coming up from behind you). To your left is the fish market.

There are excellent views from the harbour – remember to carry your camera

2 Fish Market

The market was built in modernist style in the 1920s on the remains of a bastion from the Renaissance city walls. This is a great place to take in the local atmosphere as people shop for dinner.

From the market doorway turn left and you will see the massive façade of the Església des Carme directly ahead.

3 Església des Carme

18th-century Església des Carme is the largest church in the city. The adjoining cloisters now house the fresh fruit and vegetable market and the extensive collection of artefacts of the Hernandez Mora Museum.

Retrace your path across the square and when you reach the top of the Ses Voltes turn left up the narrow Portal de Mar. At the next intersection turn right into Plaça Constitució and you will find the entrance to Església de Santa Maria on the right.

4 Església de Santa Maria

The interior of the church contrasts a minimalist nave with a 'flouncy' Baroque altar and side chapels. It is famed for its huge organ and there are recitals daily at 11am throughout the summer.

From the doorway of the church turn right and on the north side of the square you will find the ornate Ajuntament or Town Hall.

5 Ajuntament

The Ajuntament was built in 1612 and the original structure was given a Baroque facelift in the following century. The main meeting rooms have impressive and colourful period décor.

Leave the square along c/Isabel II with the Ajuntament on your right. This is a major artery lined with fine mansions. You will walk past the Gobierno Militar building on the left before the façade of the Església de Sant Francesc appears ahead.

6 Església de Sant Francesc

Visit the Chapel of the Immaculate Conception within the church.

Completed in 1752, the intricate decoration is Churrigueresque in style.
Next door to the church is the Museu de Menorca.

7 Museu de Menorca

The island's showcase of archaeological and historical artefacts lies in its ancient remains. Enjoy the Baroque cloisters that were built as part of the greater Franciscan monastery complex.
From the entrance to the museum turn right and take c/ es Frares to the intersection on c/ s'Arraval one block ahead. Turn right here and you will see the immense Port St Roc further down the street.

8 Port St Roc

Port St Roc is the last remaining section of the medieval city wall that once protected the town.

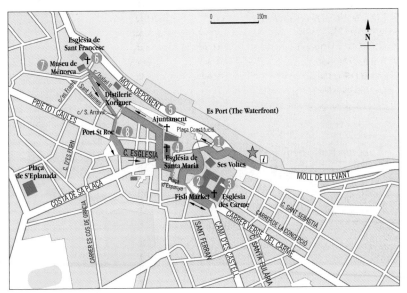

Maó Harbour

The magnificent inlet that serves Maó has been a focal point for seafarers over the centuries. Where once fleets of naval military ships plied the waters, today you can see an army of pleasure boats. 5km long and up to 1km wide, it holds several attractions along its shores, and a number of companies offer boat trips from here.

The British barracks in Maó

This is still a commercial port with a few industrial works, shipyards and the commercial docks situated inland from the city on the south side of the inlet. Day trippers can take boat cruises from the main dock in the heart of Maó (see p41) while the pleasure cruisers and yachts line the quayside to the east of the town along Moll de Llevant.

The entrance to the harbour was first fortified in the mid-16th century when the Ottoman threat from the east was at its height and both Maó and Ciutadella were attacked. Fort Sant Felip was a 'state-of-the-art' complex for its time but, in many ways, rather than protecting the population, it increased the value of Menorca to the forces who

The harbour is flooded with pleasure cruisers and yachts

coveted the island and in particular this safe harbour. When the Spanish destroyed the fort in 1782 they did so as much to render the place less attractive to other power-brokers.

It was the British, or rather the British Royal Navy, who made the inner harbour what it is today. They saw the advantage of this deep sheltered inlet even before they took possession of Menorca, and pushed for landing and watering rights with the Spanish Crown in the 1660s.

As rivalries between the European powers continued, helped by dynastic wrangling across the continent, it became imperative for the Royal Navy to secure a safe passage through the Mediterranean. Menorca was one of a series of staging posts from Gibraltar to Malta that gave Britain leverage in many pan-European disputes and power struggles.

While the city of Maó was allowed to develop relatively organically – in response to the administrative duties of the capital bestowed upon it by the British (and the resulting economic opportunities), other areas of the inlet were totally restructured to accommodate warships and the huge garrison needed to cater to this massive fleet.

Supplies were of paramount importance. Fresh food needed to be transported from the island's interior, stored and loaded. The wooden ships needed constant attention and repair, so dry docks were needed. Meanwhile smiths would be hard at work making horseshoes for the ground transport, nails for the ships and repairing the hoops of barrels.

The final decision that had to be taken was where to keep the supplies of cannon and gunpowder that the naval guns needed in times of war. The British chose a site on the north shore of the island and erected a large and secure arsenal with waterside access in the shape of a polygon, incorporating the small harbour island of de Pinto to complete the structure. Today it is not possible to visit the arsenal but you can get a good view of the buildings and the layout on the Maó harbour boat cruise (*see pp62–3*).

The inlet was a popular subject for Menorcan painters, and the changing landscape along the harbour through the different eras can be viewed in the 'paintings' section of the Museum of Menorca (*see pp42–4*) in Maó.

Cala Sant Esteve

One of the longest, narrowest and least spoilt calas on the island, Sant Esteve gives you a glimpse of what most of Menorca would have looked like before the arrival of development. Small village homes cling limpet-like to the water line; tiny fishing boats lie moored on the shoreline or tied in the centre of the

Maó Harbour

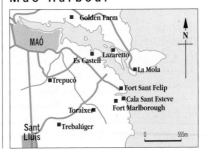

Unspoilt beauty of Cala Sant Esteve

watercourse out of harm's way; children play football along the single lane that runs around the community of brightly coloured homes; and on Sundays families get together for a long barbecue lunch and afternoon siesta.

In summer there is a large café/bar on the left just as you enter the town, which is the perfect spot for a relaxing drink or snack. The entrance to the exhibition at Fort Marlborough (*see pp54–6*) is also here, near the far end of the village (though it is not signposted as such on the approach into the cala), while the remains of Fort Sant Felip (*see pp56–7*) are set above its north shore.

Sant Esteve was given its name because it is believed that certain relics of St Stephen were landed here and these relics proved so powerful that their very presence on the island caused a large number of the Jewish population to convert to Catholicism.

Es Castell

Built by the British, Es Castell was a garrison town erected in the mid-18th century when the Royal Navy arrived for the second time.

Set on a sheltered harbour on the south shore, the garrison, then called Georgetown after King George III, sat in the protective shadow of the still-existing Fort San Felip (*see pp56–7*), just a couple of kilometres away to the southeast, which the Royal Navy used to full advantage. Fort Marlborough (*see pp54–6*) was erected to counter the changing technology of naval armaments during the mid-18th century. During the first occupation, the British had made do with a smaller garrison, S'Arraval Nova, that had grown around Fort San Felip but this was never really suitable or large enough. At the height of the British presence the place would have been bustling with tattooed sailors taking the 'King's shilling', plus an administrative team, and station personnel and their families. When the British left, the compound was taken over by the Spanish and life continued pretty much like this for Es Castell through to the end of the Franco era in the 1970s.

Today, on the face of it, there are few reminders of the founding of the town. Rows of whitewashed family homes line the streets and there is a relaxed atmosphere to the harbour front. This could be any Menorcan town until you delve a bit deeper.

At the top of the town is a large open square now called Plaça de S' Esplanada. Aside from Plaça d'es Born in Ciutadella (*see p138*), this is the biggest on the island and its size is due to the fact that it was once a parade ground for the military; it became public space after they abandoned the site in the latter part of the 20th century. All the buildings flanking the square were built as part of the original garrison headquarters. Homogenous if rather dull in style, they were the heart and soul of British military life on the island and every

Es Castell is a place to relax, away from the hustle and bustle of Maó

The Town Hall at Es Castell

Head down to the seafront and you can still see the attraction of the location to naval planners. Set around the two broad inlets of Cala Corb and Calasfonts the access was redesigned by the British to offer easy docking and maximum protection for the vessels. Today, the harbourside is home to a busy squadron of small fishing boats, and the dockside buildings house cafés and shops. The only obvious reminder of the military is a single tower on the north side of Calasfonts. Es Castell is known for its seafood restaurants and it is the place where those from the capital come for a relaxed lunch away from the tourist crowds that pack Maó's eateries.
Museu Militar. Plaça s'Esplanada.
Tel: 971 36 21 00. Open: Mon, Wed, Thur
& first Sun of the month 11am–1pm.
Admission charge.

decision would have been approved by stiffly costumed and bewigged officers sitting in offices in these buildings. The central square would have been overflowing with ceremonial pomp.

Today, the main sounds in the parade ground are those of children playing in the park set up in one corner. One side of the quadrangle houses the Es Castell town hall with its distinctive red façade, while another has Museu Militar, a small military museum. The rest of the buildings lie empty and forlorn, as though waiting for some grand purpose. The museum has artefacts, models and prints or paintings of every military era on the island, and certainly helps in the understanding of the island's complex history. Lovers of naval history will be fascinated.

Fort Marlborough

When the British took control of Menorca in the early years of the 18th century they realised that the southeastern flank of Fort Sant Felip was vulnerable, and that changes to the structure itself would not be adequate. Instead, they decided to build a totally independent fortification incorporating the latest advances in military design. It was named Fort Marlborough after Sir John Churchill, Duke of Marlborough, who was the most noted military man of the era.

The basis for the fort's impregnability was that it was built underground, cut out of rock, with access from Cala Sant Esteve (*see pp51–2*). Work started in 1710 and was completed in the mid-1720s. From the outside, the structure seems fairly simple with a featureless mound (once the site of gunnery placements) surrounded by a moat that would have held water. The fort suffered two attacks: from the French in 1756 and the Spanish in 1781. On both occasions the garrison eventually capitulated but only after prolonged sieges that diverted the attackers' attention from other targets. The small garrison of 65 men and a commander cost the enemy a lot more men, time and valuable resources. Towards the end of the 18th century, during the final British occupation, a Martello Tower – the Stuart or Penjat Tower – was added atop a nearby bluff.

The interior is a maze of seemingly endless tunnels leading off a main bore. The fort museum, set in the heart of the underground chambers, is excellent with some good high-tech displays and plenty of audio-visual exhibits that explain the history of the building and its historical context. There are also some interesting details that bring the human touch into military strategy, such as what everyday life was like for the servicemen based here. History buffs will particularly enjoy the retelling of the sieges and military action that took place here, as part of the greater power games played across Europe and the colonies by Britain, France and Spain during the late 18th and early 19th centuries.

The impregnable Fort Marlborough

Martello Tower

You can head out on the point above the fort to the Martello Tower for views across the mouth of Maó inlet and the remains of Sant Felip and Fort Isabel (*see pp57–9*).
Fort Marlborough. Cala de Sant Esteve. Tel: 971 36 04 62. Open: Tue–Sat 10am–1pm & 5–8pm, Sun 10am–1pm. Closed Mon. Admission charge.

Fort Sant Felip

It is difficult to imagine the impact that the building of Fort Sant Felip had on Menorca's reputation in the eyes of European power-brokers. Built in the mid-16th century on the orders of Charles V, the Holy Roman Emperor and the most powerful man of his era, the fort was meant as a deterrant – initially against the Ottomans – but it added value to Maó's excellent natural harbour and made it more attractive to other European nations because it could now be defended.

Fort Sant Felip stood on the south bank of the inlet with flanks out both to the west and east over the sea approaches. Unfortunately there is little left of the original structure as it was destroyed by the Spanish after they retook the island in the late 18th century. However, the site remained strategically important and today it is still a military area. On the ground it is possible to make out scant sections of what would have been massive curtain walls and arrow-shaped rivets. But we only have chroniclers' versions as to what the castle really looked like. Head to the Menorca Military Museum in Es Castell (*see pp52–4*) for more details in the form of models and paintings.

Beneath the surface there is much more going on with artillery placements in corridors and galleries where the main body of the garrison would have been housed. The labyrinth was extended over the decades with each new colonial overlord, and it is much larger than its cousin Fort Marlborough (*see pp54–6*). During the siege of 1782, it is said that over 3,500 English personnel and their families were holed up here for six months.

Fort Sant Felip. Tel: 971 36 21 00. Closed to the public except for guided tours: Jun–Sept Thur & Sat 10am; Oct–May Sat 10am. Admission charge.

La Mola

La Mola is the general term for the nub of land that occupies the far northeastern corner of the inlet at the mouth of the harbour. Just as on the south shore, this area was extremely important strategic military land, and it is covered with fortifications. Fortalesa de Isabel II, built here by the Spanish in the 18th century, had little military value but added greatly to national confidence at a time when Spain was losing its influence. It was a feared political prison throughout Franco's regime and for decades after was off-limits to the public. It was reopened

The 381mm (15 inch) Vickers battery gun at Fort Isabel II

A view over Fort Isabel II

to great aplomb as Menorca's most impressive new attraction in the early 2000s.

The fort was built to counter a specific threat in the late 1840s. The British still had a strong presence in the Mediterranean and the French were expanding into North Africa. Between these two strong powers lay the Balearics, and the Spanish felt uneasy that one or the other would take the islands. Unfortunately, the military planners did not account for the advancements in artillery that took place at this time and the castle took so long to build – 25 years – that it was outdated even before it was finished.

The fort was named after Queen Isabel II in honour of her visit to the garrison soon after it was completed.

Once through the impressive entry portal, a series of numbered panels offer more information about various sections of the fortifications, the bulk of which face southwest overlooking the approaches from the Maó inlet rather than out to sea. The hornwork and redoubt at the southwesternmost corner are, without doubt, the most impressive surface features, with strong sturdy walls and small holes at every gunning placement. There is symmetry in the design, which harks back to the Martello Tower that was so effective a hundred years earlier. There are excellent views across the inlet to the capital from here.

Fort Isabel II also has impressive underground galleries leading to gunning placements in the curtain walls.

The Loop-holed Gallery is a long row of interconnected gunning rooms that must have been extremely claustrophobic and hot for the soldiers on duty. The walking tour leads you directly through the structure.

Out to the eastern section of the fort, you will emerge into open air again and stroll past several modern barracks used in the late 20th century to reach the Isabel II's tour de force, a 381mm (15 inch) Vickers battery gun still embedded in its position. For more details of the fort, see Fort Isabel II walk (*see pp64–5*). The whole tour with accompanied audio information takes about two and a half hours with quite a lot of walking, but the fort offers a minibus service between the Loop-holed Gallery, the Vickers gun and the ticket office in the afternoons, between 1pm and 3pm.

Much of the rest of La Mola is open ground, and it is a favourite place for locals to come for a spot of fishing or just to sit and watch the boats enter and leave the harbour. You could bring a picnic and find a quiet spot for a relaxed lunch.
Fort Isabel II.
Tel: 971 41 10 66.
www.fortalesmola.com
Open: Jun–Sept Tue–Sun 10am–8pm; May & Oct 10am–6pm; Nov–Apr 10am–2pm.
Admission charge.
Daily trips from the port at Maó with Yellow Catamarans (tel: 971 35 23 07).

Lazaretto and the islands
Several islands dot the Maó inlet. The largest of these is Lazaretto or Ille de Llatzeret, just inland from La Mola. In fact the island was attached to the spit of La Mola until the early 20th century

Sightseeing at the fort

The small island of Illa Quarentena

The Loop-holed Gallery at Fort Isabel II

when a channel was cut to separate the two, with the purpose of providing a safe approach for ships arriving at Fort Isabel II. Llatzeret was the site of a huge hospital for infectious diseases that looks every bit as imposing as the fortress nearby. The hospital closed in 1917 after which it became a holiday complex for public health workers. Newly refurbished, today it is also a conference centre.

The smallest of the islands, Illa Quarentena sits just beside Llatzeret. Officially named Illa Plana, the unofficial names arises because for many years it was a quarantine station where people would be forced to wait a certain length of time (traditionally 40 days, hence the word quarantine after *quarante* the Latin word for forty) to ascertain that they had no communicable diseases. This was a common practice among the island's communities in the wake of the devastating Black Death outbreaks. Later it became the first American base in the Mediterranean.

Finally, there is the Illa del Rei or King's Island, so called because Jaume II landed here in 1287 after he had taken Menorca from the Moors. Illa del Rei is also called 'blood island' by the local people because this is where the British built their military hospital.

Golden Farm

This handsome colonial mansion, officially known as Sant Antoni, sits high on the north bank of the inlet. It is thought that the house was Lord Nelson's billet when he was in charge of the naval company here for a short time during the 1798–1802 British occupation of the island. At the time, rumours of his affair with Lady Hamilton were rife and locals were sure that she joined him here to carry on their illicit relationship. However, it is highly unlikely that she travelled to Menorca, let alone stayed with Nelson at the mansion. Nelson himself was rarely here, being much more concerned about the fate of the Hamilton family in Naples on the Italian west coast. He even refused to return to the island when it was directly threatened by French naval forces in 1799.

The house is not open to the public. The best views of it are from the harbour cruise (*see pp62–3*).

Fishing boats moored at Illa Quarentena harbour

Boat Tour: Maó Harbour

Boats depart daily from the embarkation point at Plaça de la Miranda (the base of the Costa de Ses Voltes) for a tour of one of the world's most famous natural harbours. Some companies such as the Rutas Martimas de la Cruz (*tel: 971 35 07 78*), offer glass-bottomed boats so that you can watch the sea life as well as what's happening along the shoreline.

Time: 1 hour and 15 minutes.

Distance: 10km.

1 Plaça de la Miranda

As you leave the embarkation point at Plaça de la Miranda, you will be able to see the pleasure yachts lining the quayside to the east, and the Xoriguer Distillery housed in old portside warehouse buildings to the west.

The boat will first cross to the north bank of the inlet at one of its narrowest points.

2 The Naval Base

From here you will get your best view of the old British arsenal and naval base, where all the cannon, gunpowder and other armaments were stored. The compound still maintains its 18th-century layout and the Neo-classical buildings still look neat and tidy.

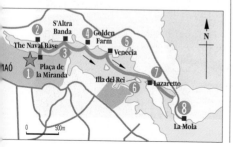

The boat will now move east slowly along the north shore out towards the sea. Just a little way along you will see a point of land jutting out into the inlet.

3 S'Altra Banda

S'Altra Banda was initially a popular place for the people of Maó to relax. Eventually, a number of villas were built here by wealthier families. The most famous buildings are the banyars de pedra or bathing houses, built in the 19th century with the lower storeys in the water so that ladies could swim without being seen.

A few minutes further east you will see Golden Farm come into view.

4 Golden Farm

This fine 18th-century mansion still has an imposing presence. It is said that Lord Nelson stayed here when he was in charge of the garrison in the 1790s.

Nearby is an unusual building.

5 Venecia

Venecia or Pequeña Venecia (Little Venice) is a single whitewashed house sitting on rocks in the shallows. It was so named because, with its feet in the water, it reminded local people of homes in Venice.

Look away from the coast from here and you will see the smallest island to the southeast, Illa del Rei.

6 Illa del Rei

In 1287 Illa del Rei was pushed centrestage when Jaume II landed here to proclaim the Islamic era on the island. The British later used it as the site for their military hospital; the Americans arrived in the 1820s.

Move on to the larger island behind Illa del Rei, Lazaretto.

7 Lazaretto

The buildings here look like fortifications but they actually housed a hospital for contagious diseases. The walls were built very high because it was thought that diseases were carried in the air, and that the walls would contain the illnesses inside.

The boat will travel on through the narrow artificial channel that was cut to separate Lazaretto from La Mola in the early 20th century, and then you will get your first view of the fort Isabel II.

8 La Mola

The fort at La Mola on the northern mouth of the Maó inlet looks impressive, but it was built using outdated design and was vulnerable as soon as it was inaugurated. During Franco's era it was used as a prison for the dictator's political enemies.

Glass-bottomed boat tours leave from Maó harbour

Walk: Fortalesa Isabel II

The Fortalesa Isabel II at La Mola is Menorca's newest historical attraction. Sections of the huge castle have been spruced up and an excellent multilingual audio accompaniment has been added, which offers a historical and architectural background to each of the numbered areas. If you have an interest in castles and forts, you will really enjoy this itinerary.

Distance: 3km.

Time: 2½ hours.

1 Queen's Gate

The entry point of the fort, Queen's Gate, is one of its finest features. Queen Isabel visited in 1860 and the castle, originally Fortalesa La Mola, was renamed Fortalesa Isabel II in her honour.

Once through the gate, the ticket office is on the left. You can get fuller details of the tour, plus background information here. From the ticket office the route leads down to the southern curtain walls and a subterranean gallery before heading north to the Hornworks.

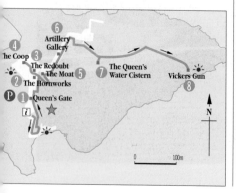

2 Hornworks

The Hornworks, with 54 cannon emplacements, were the fort's last line of defence.

Surrounding the Hornworks is The Redoubt.

3 The Redoubt

The Redoubt – from the Medieval Latin *reductus* or 'refuge', is a tiny 'fort within a fort'. The role of the building was to allow the company somewhere defendable to retreat to, should the main walls be breached.

Walk through The Redoubt and into a small square. Across the square, up the ramp is the Coop.

4 The Coop

The Coop or Caponera was a forward position that faced inland towards Maó rather than out to sea, because this was considered the flank where it was easiest to attack from as the seaward side was too rocky.

Retrace your steps past The Redoubt and walk past the reservoir. Proceed down the ramp into the moat of the pincer, a part of the castle designed to trap attackers in crossfire.

5 The Moat

The moat is now empty but was once an integral part of the defences.
From the base of the moat follow the bronze arrows to the Loop-holed or Artillery gallery, reached through a circular tower.

6 Artillery Gallery

The Artillery Gallery is a long line of gun emplacements linked by a narrow tunnel. This was the integral defence of the curtain wall facing Maó but there is no view to the outside except through the gunnery slits in the walls.
The gallery is several hundred metres long after which you emerge into the open air once more at the Princess Tower. The route now heads east out across the open

land of the La Mola peninsula. After a couple of minutes you will find the water cistern on the right.

7 The Queen's Water Cistern

This huge structure stored water and could keep the fort self-sufficient for many weeks in time of siege.
Continue to walk seaward and you will reach the final defences.

8 The 15-inch Vickers Gun

The 15-inch Vickers gun was added to the defences during the 20th century. It represents the development in military systems and tactics after the 1850s, when the fort was built.
There is a café here, so you can spend some time contemplating the view before walking via the marked path across the headland back to the ticket office, or waiting for the minibus to take you back to your starting point.

The tower and battlements of Fort Isabel II (Fortalesa Isabel II)

When the British gained control of Menorca they found an impoverished island struggling to feed itself.

Power was in the hands of a small number of patrician families who seemed to have cared little for the working population and simply wanted to extract taxes from them.

The plight of the local people was not normally high on the list of priorities of the colonial authorities but one exceptional individual Richard Kane, Deputy Governor and then Governor during the first occupation, happened to be the right man in the right place. He saw that there were easy solutions to many of the problems and set about introducing a sea of changes that would have an immense effect on the lives of the ordinary people. Kane's actions were not always altruistic because he had a British garrison to manage and feed. However, he left behind 'a legacy of justice and honour' where there had

been none, according to his biographer Janet Sloss, and he is still remembered with fondness by Menorcans.

Firstly, Kane assessed Menorca's poor-quality animal stock and had healthy Friesian cattle shipped out from the UK; without these, it is debatable whether Menorcan cheese (see pp118–19) would ever have achieved the quality and quantity it has today. He also ordered new seed stock to replenish the poor crops for both fodder and human food, and drained the marshes in the river basin close to Maó to increase the acreage of good-quality soil close to his garrison headquarters.

Another area he tackled was the poor transport infrastructure on the island. There was no main route linking the major towns and it was impossible to transport goods, even fresh crops, from the hinterland. Kane commissioned a road – known as Camí d'en Kane – that linked Maó with Ciutadella in the west for the first time.

Fresh water was also an issue. Though many of the buildings were designed to capture rainwater, there was no communal facility and there were frequent outbreaks of disease due to the lack of fresh water for drinking and washing. Kane approved the building of a huge cistern

close to the town of Es Mercadal in the centre of the island, and paid for it himself.

The second and third periods of British occupation, however, were far less constructive. General Johnston who was Governor between 1763–82 was a strident authoritarian, and his hard-handedness and distrust soured what had in the earlier years been a mutually beneficial relationship.

Richard Kane

Richard Kane was born in Ireland in c1662 and made military service his life, reaching the rank of Brigadier General. He was singularly successful as a commander under the Duke of Marlborough, and wrote a training and tactics manual that was influential for decades.

The prestigious job in Menorca was a just reward for his loyalty and organisational skill. Though he was temporarily transferred to manage the defence of Gibraltar against a Spanish force in the 1720s, he returned to Menorca and was still in office on the island when he died in 1736.

For more details on the life of Kane, get hold of a copy of *Richard Kane Governor of Menorca* by Janet Sloss. ISBN 0-9508153-5-7 (in paperback) *www.bonaventura.free-online.co.uk*

Facing page and above: The British barracks in Es Castell

Southeastern Menorca

The small region to the south of the capital has some of the prettiest landscapes on the island. Hundreds of neat whitewashed traditional *llocs* or farms sit amongst rolling land surrounded by vines and carpeted with vibrant bougainvillea.

The ancient Menorcans also loved it here, and some of their most dramatic legacies are to be found hidden behind high stone walls or standing sentinel in fields at the roadside.

This is a prosperous agricultural area of the Balearics, but also provides some of the most upmarket tourist development in small calas around the mostly rocky coast. Resorts like Punta Prima and S'Algar on the east coast provide the focus for boat trips and diving schools, and offer restaurants and bars in abundance. On the south coast a string of smaller and lower-key resorts line the bays. The rocky coastline backed by mature pines and dotted with villas is exceptionally alluring.

A string of small hamlets – the 'Bini's' – sit just inland from the coast. You will pass from one to the other without really noticing the boundaries, and each has a route leading down to the southeastern coast.

This small region is easy to explore by car; but the gentle undulations also offer excellent cycling along roads of a good standard. Everything is easy to find and within close proximity, and it is only around 20 minutes from Maó.

Basílica des Fornàs de Torelló

This rather underwhelming ruin is one of very few early Christian sites left in Menorca and, as such, forms an important architectural site. Most of the others were destroyed by the Vandals who, although also Christians, were an Arian sect who had different beliefs from the mainstream Christian tenets of worship (*see box*).

Built in the 5th or early 6th century the basilica stands on the site of an impressive late Roman villa. The original Roman mosaic floors were incorporated into the church and make a tremendous impact. The overall quality of the work is high and includes scenes featuring influences from Roman Africa, plus verdant foliage and peacocks. Close to the nave there is a scene depicting two lions facing the tree of life. Of the church only the base plan of the three original aisles and the apse are *in situ* but this allows you to envisage the overall floor plan. It is amazing to think that the whole building remained undiscovered or unappreciated until 1956.

Close by is the Talayot de Torellónet Vell, the highest ancient structure on the island with walls of finely chiselled stone. The tower is the only one to sport a window, but archaeologists now have a theory that this was a later addition. It

Talayot de Torellónet Vell

Southeastern Menorca

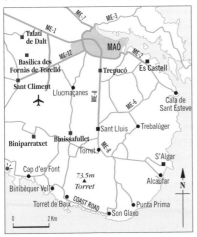

has now been usurped by the airport authorities and is equipped with high-tech equipment to facilitate landings and takeoffs. The surrounding land was the site of a Bronze Age smelting plant. Archaeologists have discovered remains of the equipment and shards of molten metal plus a small statue that may have been a ritual object.

Basílica des Fornàs de Torelló. Off the link road between the ME-1 and the Maó/Sant Climent Road, close to the airport. No phone. Open: Mon–Sat 10am–sunset, Sun 10am–1pm. Admission charge.

Binibèquer Vell

This award-winning development on the south coast is one of the turning points in the tourist market on

Tourists exploring Binibèquer Vell

The white-washed 'village' of Binibèquer Vell

Menorca. A whitewashed Mediterranean 'village' of low-rise hotels and apartment complexes designed by Spanish architect Antonio Sintes, the concept was to recreate the lines and features of a traditional fishing village while incorporating 21st-century holiday accommodation. The design plan with its soft lime-washed walls, stone steps, archways, wooden balconies and a mass of verdant landscaping, enhances the landscape rather than detracts from it, and the complex seems to tumble down the hillside into the azure water of Caló d'en Fust with its rocky outcrops.

Binibèquer Vell was a major departure from the high-rise accommodation that predominated in the whole of Spain in the 1970s, when it was conceived and built. The success of the concept helped

Menorca shift emphasis to higher-quality, lower-rise accommodation that has since sprung up around the coast.

The village is a real pleasure to explore. The narrow alleyways lead to small cottages each with a colourful door or terrace replete with local ceramics or a somnolent cat; there is a wealth of tiny details to discover around every whitewashed corner, including traditional chimneys. Every building has something a little different. Along the waterfront cala there are tiny boutiques set amidst cafés and bars – browsing is a pleasure.

Perhaps the only downside here is the lack of a decent stretch of sand to lay your towel out. Much of the sunning and bathing is done on rocks or concrete lidos.

A sign for Binibèquer Vell

Reptilian Home
The Illa de l'Aire offshore from Punta Prima is the home of the black lizard, a unique species that survives only here. Unlike many other wild reptiles, these black lizards are used to seeking food from human beings who visit the island and will approach in groups rather than running away. Lizard lovers should arm themselves with bread or other edibles!

A view of pretty Binissafullet

The parish church with a Neo-classical façade in Sant Lluis

Binissafullet

The taula at Binissafullet is a single-feature site but it sits in one of the prettiest parts of the island and doesn't require any walking from the car park. Enjoy the cluster of whitewashed traditional *llocs* or farm complexes, that have been renovated. Some are now holiday homes for British and German expats; others are excellent agrotourism complexes; and the rest remain a vibrant working part of the rural lifestyle.
At the southern junction of the Llucmaçanes road and the road north from Binibèquer Vell.
Open: 24 hours. Admission free.

Punta Prima

One of the two main tourist developments in the southeast, Punta Prima is set in the very southeastern corner of Menorca. The resort has a good range of holiday hotels, bars and some long stretches of sandy beach, and is popular among those who want the action of Maó close at hand. The choppy seas on this part of the island attract Menorca's windsurfers but swimming can be dangerous if you venture too far from the shore because of the deep currents between the land and the Illa de l'Aire offshore. There is a flag system in operation; red means don't go! Over the centuries, the dangerous waters have resulted in numerous shipwrecks that now make excellent diving sites.

S'Algar

Along with Punta Prima, S'Algar provides much of the holiday accommodation in the region and has been established since the earliest days of tourism on the island. Here this tends to be family villas set in verdant gardens, rather predictable but certainly better than high-rise faceless towers. The resort faces south on a sheltered bay with a reasonable swimming beach. The prettier resort of Cala d'Alcaufar lying less than a kilometre south around the coast, set around a narrow curved inlet protected by the remains of a stone tower, has lower key development and has more character.

From S'Algar you can take an easy walk (around 1½ hrs) to Barranc de Rafalet, where the rocky outcrops offer some fine views.

Sant Climent

This tiny village was founded in 1817 on the site of a 13th-century chapel commissioned by Jaume II, and it is now unfortunately in the final approach path of the airport. Not a place to spend your whole holiday and of the original chapel there is no sign, but stop for a little while to admire the neo-Gothic replacement erected in 1889.

The village also has one of the last remaining 'el cos' roads – an extra wide section of town road used for horse and donkey races. At various points along the track you will see narrow steps up the sides of the stone walls, that allowed the spectators to climb to the top for a better view. A plaque in Spanish marks the site.

'El cos', at the start of the route to Binidalí. Open access. Admission free.

The windmill (Molí de Dalt) in Sant Lluis now houses the Ethnology Museum

The ancient site of Talatí de Dalt

Sant Lluis

Built by the French when they took the island in 1756, Sant Lluis was a military town and erected according to the new principles of town planning on a grid of straight streets and 90° intersections, totally different from the organic expansion of the older settlements on the island with their narrow curved alleyways. The original town consisted of 18 blocks but the modern town has expanded well beyond this. The predominantly Breton sailors of the French fleet were garrisoned here under the Count of Lannion. Today, though many of the buildings have been replaced, some of the original buildings line the routes that lead to Carrer de Sant Lluis, the main thoroughfare. Their whitewashed walls bring the disparate styles and sizes together into a passable whole. The town's Neo-classical parish church was consecrated to the canonised Louis IX, after whom the town is also named. He played a pre-eminent role in the Crusades during the 13th century.

However, there are few other reminders of the French presence here. The town's **Museu Etnológic** (Ethnology Museum) is housed in the Molí de Dalt, a renovated 18th-century windmill, and it concentrates on local lifestyle and traditional practices. You will find a range of interesting old farm implements and other tools plus some pretty traditional costumes in the ethnological section. The mill was restored in 1987 and the machinery is still in working order.

Close by is a vast Italianate mansion that has seen better days but would still make a beautiful boutique hotel or grand family mansion (private property).

Museu Etnológic: Tel: 971 15 10 84.
Open: Mon–Fri 10am–2pm & 6–8pm,
Sat–Sun 10am–1pm. Admission charge.

Talatí de Dalt

One of Menorca's major Talayotic remains, Talatí de Dalt is probably the best preserved of its ancient sites. It has been thoroughly excavated in the years since 1997 and has yielded a vast amount of information for archaeologists. Because this site offers a complete village, all sorts of activities relating to the domestic and monumental buildings are beginning to be put into context, sowing the seeds for greater understanding of this mysterious people.

The settlement is now thought to have had a population of around 100 people in its heyday, around the 3rd century BC, when it was an important trading town with links to Carthage. It was well populated until the Romans took the island in the 2nd century BC and continued to offer shelter throughout the first millennium and until the Moorish rout in the 13th century, but by that time it had been in decline for a few centuries and constituted little more

Give me shelter

There are few places on the island where the traditional dry-stone walls look so beautiful. These chest-high structures are not just good to look at but have always played an important role in the health of farming on Menorca. In winter the Tramuntana wind blows from the north and without the walls, delicate crops and valuable soil would disappear south across the Mediterranean.

The taula at Talatí de Dalt

than meagre accommodation for human beings or animals.

The structures here form a loose semicircle surrounded by the remains of an original megalithic curtain wall. The site includes natural and artificial caves used, it is thought, as burial chambers or reliquaries, and a number of Talayotic houses of varying sizes, some with sophisticated hypostyle chambers and flagstone roofs. One house was found to have domestic artefacts dating from the middle of the Talayotic period through the Phoenician and Roman influences with a layer of shards of Arabic pottery at the top – taking us through the whole gamut of civilisation at the site.

The whole complex is fascinating to anyone who has an interest in ancient history. The two main attractions for the lay person are the huge main talayot or stone tower (made of finely worked trapezoid stones) and the impressive taula, surrounded by a wall of standing stones. This was used for rituals that have yet to be fully explained.

4km west of Maó just south of the ME-1. No telephone. Open: daily 10am–sunset. Admission charge.

Torret de Baix

A small tourist resort, part of the Binibèquer Vell line of small resorts, is based around the remains of an old stone tower. The small inlet in the resort

The taula at Trepucó has a 4.2m high supporting stone!

still has a handful of traditional waterside Menorcan fishermen's houses with rooms above for the family and a basement for the two or three-man boat with a concrete or stone ramp leading into the water. This inlet with its pine trees and lido bathing is one of the most photographed on the island.

Trepucó

It is known that Trepucó was a large Talayotic settlement and an important trading centre close to the inlet at Maó. Today, however, the excavated site is a smaller site than the one at Talatí de Dalt (*see pp75–6*). The quality of the buildings here makes up for the lack of quantity, and the site is well worth visiting. The dramatic taula is probably the finest on the island with a single supporting stone of 4.2m, and it is surrounded, in close proximity, by a circle of other buildings whose walls rise to at least waist level. There are two talayots on the site but the larger one suffered at the hands of the French who put a gun emplacement on top of it. The French also built characteristic arrowhead curtain walls around the tower – state-of-the-art fortifications at that time.

Tombs at the ancient Talayotic site of Talatí de Dalt

Archaeologists believe that there were four towers in ancient times. However the other two are probably field walls or farm buildings today.

1.5km south of Maó. No telephone. Open access. Admission charge when office is manned.

Rise above it all

Airmenorca runs 'discover Menorca' packages where you can head up above the island and take in its major attractions from the air. Because the island is small, you can explore much of the coastline in an hour, so the price is affordable. Prices are per person for the standard tour; or you can charter a plane if you want to see something specific. *Tel: 670 32 66 35. www.airmenorca.com*

Happy Landings

When extensions were made to Menorca airport in the wake of the development of mass tourism, some ancient remains had to be moved or destroyed in the process. Just beside the airport terminal is Biniparratxet Petit, excavated and moved to its present site in 1995. The reconstruction is of a complete Talayotic house with a hypostyle chamber. The numerous finds excavated at the time are now housed in the National Museum of Menorca.

Drive: Southeastern Menorca

This compact corner of the island, a combination of the ancient and the modern has some excellent coastal scenery and lots of places to stop and admire the view, shop, or stop for a drink or lunch.

Distance: 36km.

Time: 4 hours.

Start from the centre of Maó following signs for Trepucó. This is not signposted directly from the centre of town; find the outer ring road and if travelling east towards Es Castell take a right turn on the next roundabout after the Sant Lluís roundabout. The site is 1.5km down this narrow lane.

1 Trepucó

The dramatic taula is probably the finest on the island with a single supporting stone of 4.2m and it is

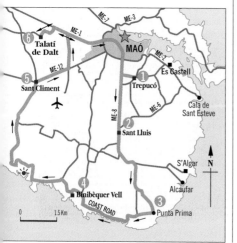

surrounded by a circle of other domestic buildings.

Leave the site and head back to the ring road at Maó. Turn left and then left again at the next roundabout. You are now on the ME-8 to Sant Lluís, 5km ahead.

2 Sant Lluís

Sant Lluís is a military town founded by the French. Enjoy the parish church and the Ethnology Museum housed in the town's old windmill.

Leave Sant Lluís by travelling south out of town on the ME-8 in the direction of Alcaufar and Punta Prima. After 2km the road splits; you will take the right fork to Punta Prima.

3 Punta Prima

Punta Prima is a well-established resort with a vast stretch of sandy beach. Just offshore is the Ill de l'Aire, now a protected nature reserve. You can take a short boat trip here or walk along the coast.

Leave Punta Prima travelling west following signs for Biniancolla and Binibèquer. You will eventually reach the main coast road. Travel on with the sea on your left. The route runs past some pretty tiny inlets with concrete bathing lidos and the occasional traditional fisherman's cottage set against the water's edge. After 4km you'll reach Binibèquer Vell.

4 Binibèquer Vell

A mock-Mediterranean fishing village that sets the tone for Menorca's modern approach to tourist development. Enjoy exploring its narrow alleyways.

Leave the resort by continuing west along the coast road through Binissafuller and Cap d'en Font. The road passes through ever-expanding tourist development with half-built villas and apartment estates and planned urbanisation. Eventually 6km from Binibèquer Vell the road turns inland and it is 4.5km to Sant Climent.

5 Sant Climent

The neo-Gothic church erected in 1889 dominates the town square and the village has one of the last remaining 'el cos' roads – an extra wide section of town road used for horse and donkey races – in Menorca.

Leave Sant Climent travelling east in the direction of Maó. At the next major junction (1.5km) turn left at the roundabout and left again at the next roundabout in the direction of Ciutadella. After 1km you will see a sign left for Talatí de Dalt.

6 Talatí de Dalt

This settlement had a population of around 100 people in its heyday. The taula is the only one on the island to be supported by a second stone T, and one house was found to have domestic artefacts dating from the middle of the Talayotic period through the Phoenician and Roman to the Moorish era.

From the Talatí de Dalt return to the main road and turn right, following the main island road, the ME-1, back to Maó.

Punta Prima's sandy beach attracts many visitors

Drive: Discovering Menorca's ancient past

Wandering from one ancient site to another makes for a great day of exploration. You will find yourself in a whole range of locations and environments, and you will be able to take in the full gamut of Menorca's differing landscapes.

Time: 7 hours.

Distance: 110km.

Leave Maó heading south following signs for Trepucó. This is not signposted directly from the centre of town but find the outer ring road and if travelling east towards Es Castell turn right at the next roundabout after the Sant Lluis roundabout. The site is 1.5km down this narrow lane.

1 Trepucó

Trepucó is a village site (*see p77*).

From the site, retrace your steps and return to the Sant Lluis roundabout taking the route to this town. Once there, follow signs for Binibèquer Vell out to the southwest, but just as you are about to take the left turn for the coast drive about 150m further on you will find the site of Binissafúllet on the right.

Talatí de Trepucó

2 Binissafúllet

Binissafúllet offers a single taula (*see p72*).

Leave Binissafúllet by taking the narrow cross-country lane running to the east of the site directly north to Llucmaçanes (sometimes spelt Llucmassanes). In the village take the left fork signposted Sant Climent. When you reach the Maó/Sant Climent road after 1.5km, turn left, then right at the next large roundabout. After 1.5km you will reach the ME-1. Take the Ciutadella direction. After 2.5km you will see a sign left to Talatí de Dalt.

3 Talatí de Dalt

Talatí de Dalt was a large ancient village (*see p75–6*).

Return to the ME-1 and continue in the direction of Ciutadella. After 3km you will see a narrow turning to the right with a small signpost to Rafal Rubi situated just off the route.

4 Rafal Rubi

The Rafal Rubi site has twin navetas (*see p113*).

Continue westward towards Ciutadella. After 6.5kms you will be approaching Alaior. Take the first Alaior exit off the bypass road and turn south going under this bypass and on to a country lane with signposts to Cala'n Porter. After 4km the signs for Torralba d'en Salord will come into view.

5 Torralba d'en Salord

Torralba d'en Salord village has the biggest taula in Menorca (*see p117*).
Retrace your route to the Alaior bypass and continue on towards Ciutadella. Travel through Es Mercadal and Ferreries enjoying the open views around the towns. 8km after leaving Ferreries, look out for small brown signs to the Torre Llafuda on the left. The road is little more than a track and is easy to miss (it is around 1km after the houses of Ses Tavernes).

6 Torre Llafuda

Torre Llafuda is one of Menorca's least studied sites (*see p135*).
Link up with the ME-1 again towards

Ciutadella. After 2kms you will see a sign on the left to Torre Trencada. Follow the narrow walled road for a kilometre, then turn left, and it is 2.5km to the site.

7 Torre Trencada

Torre Trencada is a village site (*see p135*).
Return to the main ME-1 by turning right out of the site and then right again at the next crossroads. You are almost on the outskirts of Ciutadella when the car park for Naveta des Tudons comes into view on the left (around 1km from the last junction for Torre Trencada).

8 Naveta des Tudons

Naveta des Tudons is a spectacular single naveta (*see p132 & p134*).
After a hard day's sightseeing head 6km into Ciutadella and relax with a drink at the harbour.

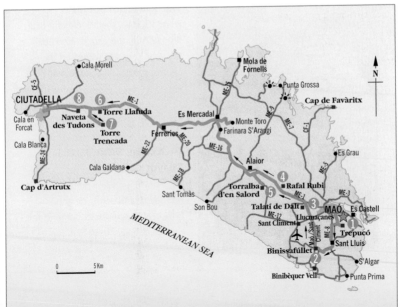

Menorca was densely populated during ancient times and these people have left a vast legacy, principally in the form of stone structures that are only now yielding their secrets to archaeologists. Some of the sites were used long after the ancient civilisations had disappeared, and show traces through the first millennium into medieval times. Many others were used as animal shelters until the advent of the science of archaeology.

THE CLASSIFICATION

The scientific community has now separated the development of early Menorcan society into separate eras. Before c1300 BC the population is known as pre-Talayotic I and pre-

Talayotic II, and after that date as Talayotic. The Talayotic era lasted until the arrival of the Romans in 123 BC.

The Pre-Talayotic People

The earliest remains so far studied have been dated 2500 BC, and until 1800 BC these have been grouped as pre-Talayotic I relating to the Chalcolithic geological era. The people lived in stone huts and adapted caves for settlements and hypogeums or burial chambers. The caves at Calascoves (see p107) and Cala Morell (see pp122–3) show the level of skill achieved by the 'cave dwellers'.

From 1800 BC to 1500 BC, the Early Bronze Age, the people are known as pre-Talayotic II and the main difference was development of the burial chambers from the pre-Talayotic I time.

The Talayotic Peoples

From 1500 BC, the Middle and Late Bronze Age, the people are known as Talayotic. This era witnessed the development of the stone mega-structures and village communities we can visit today, and were typified by elongated stone burial chambers.

TALAYOTIC STRUCTURES
Talayot

The talayot, which is omnipresent on the island (and across neighbouring Mallorca), has given its name to this race of people. These high (up to 10m) conical towers were built with cyclopean stones that stood at the highest point of the village. The exact purpose of the towers has yet to be ascertained but they could have offered protection to the village in times of danger, or acted as a meeting house for community elders. There are over 200 talayots in Menorca and many more may have existed but the stones were recycled in later eras.

Taula

The word taula means 'table' in Catalan. Standing at least shoulder height and up to a height of 4m these huge flat stones supported by one or more stone uprights were certainly not used as tables. Researchers believe that they were ritual areas, each surrounded by a horse-shoe-shaped stone wall. The latest theory is that these were a representation of a bull's head – the bull being a revered animal all across the Mediterranean basin in ancient times. The archaeologist's find of the bronze statue at Torralba d'en Salord (see p42 & pp116–17) would support this.

hewn stone mounds had interior chambers that acted as collective ossuaries. The bones of generations of Talayotic people were laid to rest in these with their precious objects. The artefacts found in navetas across the island have added a great deal to our knowledge and respect for these people. The finest example is the Naveta des Tudons (see p132 & p134) just east of Ciutadella.

Naveta

Single constructions with no surrounding buildings these huge rough-

Facing page: Naveta des Tudons near Ciutadella
Above: Talayotic graves at Torre Trencada

Northern Menorca

Menorca's northern region, the 'tramuntana', is its wild land, swept by the northern winds. It is slightly cooler than the south in summer and battered by storms in winter. Its vegetation is always low-growing and sometimes non-existent with several lunar-type landscapes adding drama to the island's diverse geographical palate.

A couple relax at Arenal d'en Castell beach resort

The north has all of Menorca's 'high' ground with three peaks reaching heights of 250m, though it is generally characterised by rolling hills and a serrated coastline of inlets and rocky peninsulas thrusting out into the Mediterranean.

Northern Menorca

It is the feeling of a wild and windswept region that is the major draw here. Much of the land is covered by the protective covenants of the Parc Naturel de S'Albufera des Grau (*see pp91–4*) so we can be sure that development will be kept to a carefully planned minimum. Nestled between the headlands are majestic untamed beaches and exceptional marshlands that welcome regular spring and autumn visitors in the form of migrating birds.

The north sees fewer visitors than the verdant 'migjorn' with its picturesque barrancas or the west with its family resorts, though upmarket Son Parc attracts golfers and Arenal d'en Castell can match any resort for holiday fun. Windsurfers flock to the bay at Fornells for the excellent conditions while gourmands head to the same place to sate their appetites on the best cuisine in Menorca, particularly the *caldereta de llangosta*, the 'king' of seafood dishes, that's the speciality here. The walking and hiking trails are an excellent way to work off a heavy lunch. Head out from any of the coastal towns or villages and before long you will reach your own private sheltered cove for a spot of swimming or sunbathing.

Addaia

Once the island's most picturesque pleasure port, the cala at Addaia has developed into a fully formed but low-key resort with rows of holiday villas that are busy in season but perhaps a bit of a ghost town the rest of the year. Just north of the bay is Na Macaret, a favoured inlet for Menorcan town-dwellers who head out here in the summer from Maó and Ciutadella. Most people have holiday homes that have been passed down through the family and it has few of the trappings of mass tourism.

Arenal d'en Castell

The north coast's largest resort, Arenal d'en Castell, is set around a wonderful horseshoe-shaped bay protected by two rocky spits that come together like crab claws just offshore. The beach has fine sand and calm waters that are great for kids but the land behind climbs steeply, which means lots of steps up and down to the beach.

There is a pretty Mediterranean low-rise holiday complex reminiscent of Binibèquer Vell (*see pp 69–71*) rising from the beach in the centre of the bay but the resort sports some pretty ugly older-style block hotels.

However, in the peak of the season it is one of Menorca's most buzzing places and has a good range of restaurants, bars and shops.

Badia de Fornells (Fornells Bay)

There is not much sand around Fornells (*see pp88–91*) but the shallow and protected waters of the Badia de Fornells south of the town offer one of the best watersports environments in Menorca, perfect for windsurfing and sea kayaking. A number of schools run

Sun, sand and fun at Arenal d'en Castell

The shallow waters of the Badia de Fornells is perfect for watersports

training courses or offer rental equipment so that whatever your skill level, you can have fun here. Sea kayakers can head out of the inlet and explore the rocky coastline along the north coast with its numerous caves and coves. The most famous, the Cova del Angleses (Cave of the English), a huge cathedral-like space, can be reached by a boat trip from Fornells during the summer.

Away from the water, the landscape around the bay is open countryside swept by the tramuntana. There are some excellent walking routes, particularly on the uninhabited eastern peninsula. The highest point, the Mola de Fornells on the eastern flank of the mouth of the inlet, rises to 122m and offers views back across the coastal plain.

Cami d'en Kane (The Kane Road)

Menorca's first reliable cross-island road was completed during the governorship of Richard Kane (*see pp66–7*) in the early 18th century. It revolutionised transport and communications on the island.

The Cami d'en Kane with its narrow width and high dry-stone walls became obsolete as time passed and transport technology improved, but instead of widening it, the Menorcans built a new faster and wider road, the ME-1 that now takes the bulk of the cross-island traffic, leaving the Kane road for those who want to take a road less travelled.

Recently the island has started to reclaim its heritage and has invested in a new asphalt surface for the road, making it even better for cycling and a smoother ride for cars. There is very little traffic on the route and you can enjoy the views of *llocs* and farmland as you travel along.

Cami d'en Kane runs west from 2.5km north of Maó on the 710 Maó/Fornells road to the outskirts of Es Mercadal. It sits north of the ME-1.

Cap de Favàritx

The most surreally beautiful spot on Menorca, Cap de Favàritx is a barren grey slate headland pointing northeastward into the Mediterranean. The earth has played a wonderful trick here, twisting and folding the sedimentary rock so that the layers lie almost vertical. This dark and foreboding spot is pounded by waves and chiselled by wind, flaking into millions of shards that blanket the surface. Standing sentinel above the spray and flotsam is the Cap de Favàritx lighthouse, to protect the ships that traverse the dangerous waters offshore.

In the last couple of decades marine archaeologists have discovered the remains of a Roman shipwreck off the point, proof of its treacherous reefs and currents. Finds brought up from the seabed include amphorae and coins that shed light on the commerce in Menorca during that era. A range of these is on display in the Museum of Menorca in Maó (*see pp42–4*).

Note: Cap de Favàritx forms part of the S'Albufera des Grau Natural Park (*see pp91–4*) and is protected land.

The Kane Road

Ermita de Fátima

One of several centres of pilgrimage in Menorca, there has been a chapel on the site of the Ermita de Fátima since the Middle Ages. However the present church was built in the 1950s. It is not an overly modern design, though in a pleasant spot on a small hillock surrounded by countryside, and it is a popular place for locals to get married.

Not open regular hours. Admission free.

Es Grau

This tiny fishing village is the most authentic coastal settlement on the island. A tiny cluster of whitewashed cottages set against glistening azure waters dotted with tiny bobbing boats, its waterfront sports small nets and lobster pots ready for tomorrow's catch.

Es Grau has its fair share of visitors but there are few places to stay, so tourism hasn't altered life or the landscape too much. This region is part of the Parc Naturel de S'Albufera des Grau (*see pp91–4*) and therefore its authenticity is not going to change in the future either. From here you can take a boat trip to the Illa d'en Colom (*see p91*); the beaches to the west are unspoilt and uncrowded – reached only on foot. It is also an easy route to the park information centre.

Fornells

Set on the banks of a large lake-like inlet, the village of Fornells is a pretty cluster

The coastline of Cap de Favàritx

IT'S THE BRITISH WAY

In 1756 the French besieged Fort San Felipe in the Maó inlet (*see pp56-7*) in the opening days of the Seven Years War. Admiral John Byng was dispatched post-haste to Menorca to sort the situation but dragged his heels, finally meeting the French fleet off Cap de Favàritx. The battle was by all accounts a draw but Byng lost confidence and retreated to Gibraltar sealing the fate of the British garrison on the island.

Byng was to pay for his reticence with his life. On his return to his homeland he was courtmartialled and then shot for dereliction of duty. This incident inspired Voltaire to comment in his novel *Candide* that 'the British needed to shoot an admiral now and then in order to encourage the others'.

The picture-perfect village of Fornells

of whitewashed buildings with their painted shutters nestling against the palm-lined waterside, a picture-perfect fishing community. This isn't a tourist resort but it is a popular anchorage for the summer yachting crowd and one of the most visited places on the island for its *caldereta de llangosta*, a mouth-watering lobster 'stew' that is the

A Flying Visit

It is worth remembering in these days of non-stop intercontinental flights that planes once had a much shorter range. France had a colony in northern Africa but its early scheduled flights by seaplane couldn't cross the Mediterranean from Marseille to Algiers in one hop, so from 1937–1939 they made regular refuelling stops in the sheltered inlet at Fornells.

Fishermen bringing in their catch at Es Grau dockside

The yachting crowd love Fornells in the summer

signature dish of Menorca. Several restaurants offer this – though it is certainly the most expensive item on the menu – in addition to a menu of delicious seafood, and you should certainly make time during your trip for a leisurely lunch here.

The village grew up around Fort Sant Antoni, built in the 1600s to protect against the Ottoman threat but now in ruins. 1500m north of Fornells, at the mouth of the inlet, is a recently renovated Martello tower built by the British in 1798 just before they departed Menorca for the last time. The **Torre de Fornells** now looks a little over-restored though it is bound to weather in time. There is a small military museum inside. In the shadow of the tower is a tiny but immaculately kept shrine, the Ermita de Loudres where the fishermen's wives still

come to offer prayers for the safe return of their husbands.

The platjas de Fornells (Fornells beaches) lie to the west of the Fornells peninsula, the best being Cala Tirant, reached by road from Salines south of Fornells town. This wild beach backed by grass-covered dunes has developed a

Caldereta de Llangosta

Every restaurant that serves this excellent seafood dish has its own particular recipe, but if you want to try making it yourself at home here is a good and trustworthy option that will provide you with an authentic result. You will need to buy a terracotta casserole to cook it in before you leave the island, as nothing else will really do!

Ingredients for four people:
2 live spiny lobsters
2 onions (finely chopped)
3 cloves of garlic (finely chopped)
Toasted dried bread
Fresh parsley
2 litres of fish broth
0.5 litre of cava brut (sparkling wine)
A drop of Spanish brandy
2 large ripe tomatoes (finely chopped with their juice)
Pepper
Salt
Olive oil

How to cook

Tie and cook the lobster in the fish broth then break into chunks (by hand is best), and set aside. In a large open terracotta casserole, fry the onion in the olive oil. When the onion is soft add the garlic and tomatoes to obtain a loose paste. Add the fish broth and then the cava and let it simmer for 15 minutes. Add the lobster and some of the parsley, then leave to simmer for an hour with the casserole open till the sauce turns rich and creamy. Stir in the brandy and serve from the casserole with a sprinkle of parsley and toasted bread.

sandy spit that protects a small marshland filled with birds, fish and reptiles.

Torre de Fornells. Open: Tue–Sat 10am–8pm, Sun 10am–2.30pm. Admission charge, free on Sun.

Illa d'en Colom (Pigeon Island)

Lying just offshore and forming part of the Parc Naturel de S'Albufera des Grau and easily accessible by boat from Es Grau the Illa d'en Colom is Menorca's largest offshore island. There are several quiet beaches to enjoy on the sheltered western shore. The British built a quarantine station here during their stewardship, which was in use until a new complex was built on the Ille de Llatzeret (*see pp59–61*) in Maó harbour. The remains make a walk into the interior worthwhile. Watch out for lizards scurrying to and fro in the undergrowth; they are a special sub-species, Lilford's wall lizard, indigenous to Menorca and pre-dating the arrival of man, but now only found on protected offshore islands.

Parc Naturel de S'Albufera des Grau (S'Albufera des Grau Natural Park)

Menorca's showcase park acts as the core of the UNESCO biosphere reserve, and

Remains of the British quarantine station at Pigeon Island

Parc Naturel de S'Albufera des Grau (S'Albufera des Grau Natural Park)

over an area of just over 5,000 hectares, covers a whole gamut of environments and ecosystems that are typical of the Tramuntana region of the island. The park was created by the people in direct response to development plans proposed in the 1970s that would have changed this part of the coast irrevocably.

The park ranges across coves and inlets from Punta de sa Galera just east of Es Grau village (*see p88*) to Punta de Mongofra, taking in the coastal waters and the offshore Illes des Porros in the west; inland it covers land up to 3km into the hinterland. The greater area is made up of a hotchpotch of different levels of 'protection' ranging from 'area of use conditional on conservation' where farmers and fishermen continue to work within agreed guidelines, to

'strict nature reserve' where there is minimal human influence.

The strictly protected areas encompass the offshore islands – Illa d'en Colom and Illes des Porros, plus two small landlocked sections, Bassa de Morella and Es Prat. There is one strict marine area in the far north, the tiny inlet of s'Estany, which is home to rare marine plants such as the manatee grass.

Much of the park's important vegetation is very low-growing including lentisk shrub and jasmine box. Even lower-growing are the socarrells, the generic name for dwarf shrubs that live in close proximity to salt water. Some of these can only be found on Menorca. The offshore waters protect acres of Posidonia – an important marine vegetation species (*see box p94*).

The main area of interest close to the park's reception centre (just west of Es Grau) is the wetland. The spring-fed freshwater lagoon covers 70 hectares and is the largest in Menorca, offering ideal conditions for waterfowl including coot and mallard, and a host of seasonal visitors. Underwater species such as eels and striped mullet abound. Wild fauna include the European pine marten and significant populations of Iberian frogs and toads. There are a couple of lookout points along the footpaths – marked routes of between 20 and 50 minutes duration – but it is probably a good idea to use binoculars to get the best view of the birdlife.

The geology of the park will interest amateur scientists. The rocks in this part of Menorca are the oldest in the

The spring-fed lagoon in the park

Walking is the best way to see the park

Balearics and include examples from the Carboniferous period (at Cap de Favàritx – *see p99*), the Mesozoic (red ferrous rocks at Es Capell del Ferro) and the Quaternary (fossils at Illa d'en Colom and Mongofra).

The areas of farmland within the boundaries that now protect flora and fauna have become an established part of Menorca's ecosystem only because of man's intervention and the traditional farming practices that have shaped the environment through the centuries. Many plants, birds and insects rely on the continuance of these traditional land uses including the growing of crops like olives and the grazing of cattle.

Much of the land around the access road to Cap de Favàritx is covered under the 'conditional' section and it is

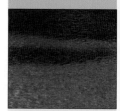

interesting to watch the gradual change in vegetation from lush farmland to vegetation more suited to dry conditions, to succulent species that need little water, to no vegetation at all by the time you reach the cape itself.
The Natural Park Information Centre. The Rodríguez Femias Reception Centre. Ctra de Maó es Grau 3.5km, Llimpa. Tel: 971 35 63 03. Open: summer Wed–Sat 9am–6pm, Sun 9am–3pm; winter Wed–Sun 9am–3pm. Admission free.

Sant Joan des Horts
Founded in the 17th century in the northern shadow of Monte Toro, this tiny church was reconstructed in 1807 in Neo-classical style and was one of Menorca's pilgrimage churches. Today, however, it is an evocative ruin surrounded by lush farmland, and the stone rose window on the façade now devoid of glass stands stark against the sky.

Son Parc
Menorca's most exclusive north coast resort, Son Parc is the site of the island's only golf course and a single fine sandy beach, both of which are set against fragrant pine forest. The bay has escaped overdevelopment up until now with only low-rise apartment blocks and few supporting restaurants and bars, which means the

Exploring the freshwater lagoon by boat

THE MEADOWS OF THE SEA

Menorca is surrounded by hectares of sea-grasses including Neptune grass and Posidonia. These form vast meadows or prairies, and scientists now know that they have played an invaluable role in maintaining the coastal landscape and the quality of the seawater.

They produce oxygen and organic materials that allow fish and other marine creatures to breathe and feed.

They stabilise the seabed and attract more sand. They temper the force of the waves, stopping the sand from being washed away.

They offer shelter and protection to several sea species including sea urchins, starfish and sea anemones, plus a breeding environment for fish.

A sheer cliff-face

beach rarely gets crowded. There is excellent walking right from the door west to Badia de Fornells or east to the resorts of Arenal d'en Castell (*see p85*), Na Macaret (*see p85*) and Addaia (*see p85*).

National Park Rules

Don't drive off prescribed routes.
Stay on the prescribed paths as walking on plants can damage delicate or rare environments.
No dogs are allowed in the park.
Don't pick the plants or stalk the animals.
Respect walls, barriers and access routes, as most National Park land is still private property.
Don't cross the dunes to the beach, as this is a fragile environment.
Camping and the lighting of fires are forbidden.
No boats to anchor in Posidonia.
Don't remove slate from the Cap de Favàritx.

An information board with a map of the park

Drive: Maó to Fornells

This short drive from the capital leads you to some of Menorca's most important wildlife habitats. It is an opportunity to do a bit of birdspotting or windsurfing before finishing the trip just in time for lunch at one of the fine restaurants in Fornells.

Time: 3 hours.
Distance: 45km.

Leave Maó on the road along the southern flank of the harbour heading west. From a roundabout at the head of the inlet, take the ME-7 signposted Fornells. After 1km take the right turn on the ME-5 towards Es Grau. After 5km there is a left turn along a country road into the heartland of the Parc Naturel de S'Albufera des Grau.

1 Parc Naturel de S'Albufera des Grau

The information office for the park is on the left a few hundred metres down this road. Stop here for information in English. Proceed to the parking area and choose one of the three walking routes around the freshwater lagoon with its prolific bird-life. There are wooden lookouts with views across the water and information panels with pictures of the birds you are likely to see.

Return to the main road and turn left, Make your way 1km or so into Es Grau. Leave your car in one of the two car parks just at the edge of the village, as access is limited.

2 Es Grau

Although there are no important attractions in Es Grau, there is always something going on: fishermen landing their catches, mending nets or repairing boats, and every little whitewashed cottage has some pretty detail to enjoy. If you want to prolong the trip you could take a boat to the Illa d'en Colom to explore this protected island or combine this drive with the walking route on page 100.

Leave Es Grau by the same route you entered and retrace your route back to the junction with the ME-7. Turn right here in the direction of Fornells. After 5km a small mound appears on the right with a stone church on the top.

3 Ermita de Fatima

The Ermita de Fatima is a relatively modern building but the history of this hermitage dates back centuries. The church is not open regular hours, though you may be lucky enough to find the guardian.

From the church continue towards Fornells. The road leads on through rolling farmland with Monte Toro, the highest point on the island up ahead on the horizon. 13km from Ermita de Fatima, the ME-7 reaches a T-junction. Take a right turn and after 1.5km you will see the Badia de Fornells on your right.

4 Badia de Fornells

Though not a lake, the narrow outlet of the bay creates similar conditions and you will normally find dozens of windsurfers plying a track across the water. The bay may also be busy with kayakers and small sailing boats.

Drive on to Fornells. Continue through the town and park at the base of the Torre de Fornells at the mouth of the inlet.

5 Fornells Watchtower

The Torre de Fornells was built by the British at the mouth of the bay during the Napoleonic era. The coastal views are spectacular with the Cap de Favàritx clearly visible to the east.

Return to Fornells.

6 Fornells

Take a pleasant stroll along the palm shaded promenade and explore the village before sitting down to a well deserved lunch.

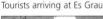
Tourists arriving at Es Grau

Drive: Menorcan Lighthouses

This island community has long realised the need to protect shipping from treacherous sections of the coastline. Lighthouses warn strangers of danger and guide locals home. This full-day tour has lighthouses as its theme, but it also leads you through some of the island's most splendid landscapes and most remote corners.

Distance: 125km.

Time: 8 hours.

Leave Maó by taking the road on the southern flank of the inlet west to a roundabout at the head of the inlet. Take the right turn signposted La Mola (the ME-3) that leads along the north of the inlet down the La Mola peninsula to Fortalesa Isabel II (see pp64–5). From the

car park here you can walk north around the fort to Punta de s'Espero.

1 Punta de s'Espero

The lighthouse at Punta de s'Espero marks Menorca's most easterly spot. *Retrace your steps to the roundabout and*

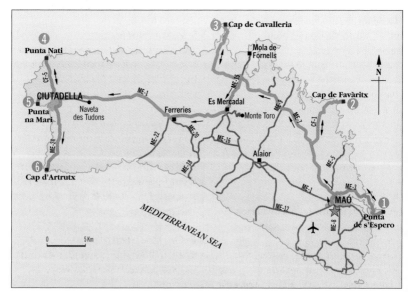

take the right turn signposted Fornells
(the ME-7). Continue along this route for
8km before taking a right turn marked
Cap de Favàritx. The road travels through
increasingly barren landscape until you
reach the cape itself.

2 Cap de Favàritx

The phare at the Cap de Favàritx is the
only splash of colour on the monotone
peninsula.
*Return to the ME-7 and turn right
following signs for Fornells. At the
T-junction with the ME-15 (12.5km)
turn right and then almost immediately
left, following the country road past
Casetes Velles and on for 4km until you
turn right for the Cap de Cavalleria.
There are only a couple of scattered llocs
on the windswept peninsula until after
8km you reach the tip.*

The lighthouse at Cap de Favàritx

3 Cap de Cavalleria

The 90m cliffs at the Cap de Cavalleria
mark the northernmost point on
mainland Menorca.
*Make your way back to the ME-15 and
turn right to Es Mercadal where you meet
the main cross-island route, the ME-1.
Follow signs to Ciutadella and after 24km
on the outskirts of the town, turn right on
the ring road signposted Cala Blanes.
Follow this narrow road until you reach a
right turning for Punta Nati.*

4 Punta Nati

Punta Nati is surrounded by barren
country dotted with huge stone
sheep-pens.
*Return to the Ciutadella ring road and
follow signs to the port, reached by going
through the centre of the town. Leave the*

port at its western end and take the first
major turning left. From here follow the
road on the north side of the inlet.

5 Punta na Mari

The diminutive lighthouse at Punta na
Mari protects this narrow inlet with the
tiny Castell de Sant Nicolau on the
southern shore.
*Return through Ciutadella to the ring
road – following signs for Maó would be
easiest at this point. When you reach the
ring road follow signs for Cala'n Bosc. The
ME-24 leads 9km to the outskirts of the
resort from where the Cap d'Artrutx is
signposted just a couple of hundred metres
ahead.*

6 Cap d'Artrutx

The Cap d'Artrutx lighthouse was built
in 1868 on this rocky southwesterly
outcrop.

Walk: Es Grau to Sa Torreta

The northern Menorcan countryside is best seen on foot. From this perspective you can appreciate the complexity of the low-growing plant life and myriad insects enjoying the pollen. This route is set in the heart of the Parc Naturel de S'Albufera des Grau and combines coastal and inland sections, finishing at Es Grau.

Time: 4 hours.

Distance: 10km round trip.

Leave your car in the car park at Es Grau and set off west around the head of the platja de Grau taking an old bridal path, Cami de Cavalls. At the far end the path rises over a low headland, the Roca des Mabres. Keep right until you reach a second smaller bay with a white house at the far end of the strand.

1 The White House

The White House is open as a café in high season and it is your last chance for refreshments. There are great views back across the bay to the village from here. *From just before the White House a well-worn path heads inland to the left, over the headland. Keep walking towards the*

A coastal cottage

Illa d'en Colom, which lies directly ahead across the es Pas channel.

2 Illa d'en Colom

You can't visit the island (*see p91*) on this walk but you can enjoy the views out across the bay from the cliff-top path.

From the cliff-top the path swings inland cutting across another headland from where the coastline opens up ahead. Walk down to the bay of Fondejador des Llanes where the route hugs the coast up to the Cala d'es Tamarells.

3 Cala d'es Tamarells

The northwestern tip of the Cala d'es Tamarells, es Colomar is marked by a ruined Martello tower, Sa Torre de Rambla, built by the British in the 18th century.

Turn left across the headland leaving the tower and coastline on your right. From here there are excellent views inland to the Parc Naturel de S'Albufera des Grau.

4 Cala sa Torreta

The park covers an area of over 5,000 hectares; but this view takes in the S'Albufera Lake, the largest freshwater ecosystem on the island.

The next bay you reach is Cala sa Torreta. Walk halfway across it before turning inland (left) through low alpine shrubland towards the ancient site.

5 Sa Torreta Site

There are fewer ancient sites in the north than in the south and Sa Torreta is probably the best of these. The site is scattered and rather overgrown but this only adds to the fun and the atmosphere.

The majestic taula at the Sa Torreta site

The naveta and other sections of the site were excavated by archaeologist M.A. Murray for Cambridge University during the early 1930s. Little more has been done since then.

The huge taula (4m) is probably the most impressive single feature; you will also find a talayot, a threshing floor and several talayotic houses amongst the wild olives.

From the site the easiest plan is to head back to Es Grau by the route you came, though there is a route leading south past the Sa Torreta lloc (farmhouse) that leads to the northern shores of the S'Albufera lake before cutting back to meet the original path at the Cala d'es Tamarells for the return to Es Grau.

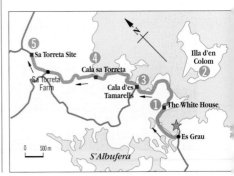

Southern Menorca

The south of Menorca, or the 'migjorn', is a vast swathe of sedimentary sandstone laid down in the Miocene period that has been carved by wind and water into a series of small valleys or barrancas running south to the sea. The pale rutted ground rock softened by holm oak, vine and olive groves offers some of the most evocative landscapes on the island, and is home to some of its prettiest resorts.

Parasols at the beach

Several barranca outlets now play host to tourist developments, from the long established Cala'n Porter to the more recent Cala de Santa Galdana, nestled around cosy fine sand beaches. Coincidentally, the migjorn also boasts Menorca's longest beaches – Son Bou and Sant Tomàs.

Even at the start of the 21st century, much of the south coast was still beyond the reach of modern vehicles, and getting about on foot brings rewards by the basketload: tiny coves, long-distance views from cliff-tops, Talayotic settlements where the only sounds are the humming of cicadas and scuttling of ground lizards.

Skyline of the medieval city of Alaior

North of the barrancas lie a string of inland towns, the major economic and administrative centres of the island. Each very different in character, they offer a chance to explore the modern Catalan heart of the island, one step removed from coastal tourism.

Alaior

Ask most Menorcans about Alaior and they will mention cheese. The town has two famous factories, Coinga and La Payesa, where you can buy direct. But there is more to the town than cheese.

Alaior was given its municipal charter by Jaume II at the start of the 14th century. Since then it has remained the administrative town for the centre of the island, and the third in line fighting for the role of capital, with Maó and Ciutadella being the first two. It was a centre of learning with a private university in 1439 and this ensured its independence until the 1700s. During the Kane governorship, land around the town was drained and it became an important fruit-producing area. Later, footwear became an important industry.

The town still sits on a medieval floor plan with a core of narrow alleyways. A couple of old windmills rise above the whitewashed cottages.

The main architectural attraction is Església Santa Eulalia (Church of Saint Eulalie), which dominates the high ground. Founded in the 14th century but reworked in the late 1600s, the exterior styling is more in keeping with military than religious architecture with two plain towers flanking the vast and plain Baroque façade. Attention is focused on the exquisite doorway with its fine carved detail, while the interior remains pure Gothic with minimal decorative elements. The former town hall or Ajuntament building is an excellent example of a Baroque palace, though the entrance patio was added in the 19th century.

A unique area in the town is Pati de Sa Lluna, a former Franciscan convent built in the late 17th century that was converted into family homes after the expulsion of the religious order in 1835. The four storeys erected around a central patio have remained unaltered and are usually festooned with family washing.

Just outside the municipality, the pilgrimage site of Sant Llorenc de Binixems holds a procession during the second week of August leading from the church into the town.

Cala'n Porter

One of Menorca's longest established tourist resorts and still a favourite, Cala'n Porter typifies why the island attracts so many tourists. Set on a narrow rocky cala with a gentle golden beach and limpid azure water, it is still stunningly attractive. The barrancas just

Southern Menorca

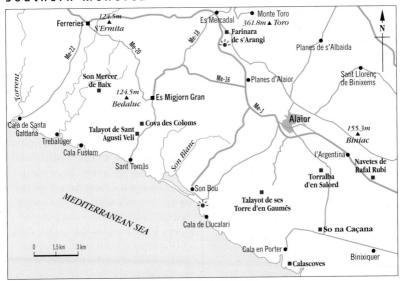

Holiday resorts dot the hillside of Cala'n Porter

inland offer typical lush southern landscapes that can be explored on foot.

The resort accommodation sits on the cliff-tops above the beach – a steep but short climb. There is a good selection of restaurants, bars and clubs to keep all ages happy, though the styling of some of the buildings is beginning to look a little dated and the roads could do with some repair.

Travel through the resort centre to reach one of the major attractions in Menorca, Cova d'en Xoroi (the Caves of Xoroi) a labyrinth of natural caverns cut high in the cliff-face overlooking the sea. After exploring the inner recesses you can look out from the cave mouths to the pounding waters below. The caves have been transformed into a playground with the addition of a bar,

café, state-of-the-art music system and neon lights. It is packed with sightseers by day and transforms into the island's best club on summer nights.
Cova d'en Xoroi. Tel: 971 37 70 64. www.covadenxoroi.com. Nightclub open: mid-May–mid-Sept nights, daytime hours daily 10.30am–6pm & 6–9pm as a bar. Admission charge.

Cala de Santa Galdana (also known as San Galdana and Santa Galdana)
Set at the base of deepest barranca on the south coast, Cala de Santa Galdana appears like a 'Shangri la' at the end of the long access road. A crescent moon-shaped beach surrounded by high cliffs and verdant foliage it is known as the 'queen of the coves' for its sheer beauty. The cala also forms the end of the

Barranc d'Algender that cuts deep into the hinterland. The mouth of the ravine is a popular anchorage for small fishing and tour boats that offer sightseeing trips along the coast.

Accommodation is a mixture of high-rise and low-rise, but the huge Sol hotel only marginally detracts from the panorama. There is a range of eateries and bars, though nightlife is pretty low-key.

The Barranc d'Algender is the largest in the migjorn. It is a mini-ravine biting 11km into the island, and it is the only one with a permanent watercourse running through it. The barranca offers a whole range of natural environments – from fully marine saltwater to brackish to freshwater – as you travel inland. The animals and plants reflect the level of salinity in the groundwater with wild holm oak and olive, the only elm trees on the island and pines in the upper reaches, and vast swathes of reed beds just inland from the resort.

The Legend of Xoroi

The caves are named after the main character in one of Menorca's best-known legends. Xoroi ('one ear') was a Moorish pirate who was shipwrecked on the island and hid out in these remote caves. After a while he became lonely and in need of some female companionship so he kidnapped a young virgin girl from her family home in Alaior.

He kept the girl prisoner for many years and she bore him several children but eventually Xoroi was discovered when he left telltale footprints during a rare winter snowstorm. When cornered he chose suicide and threw himself from the cliffs.

Cala de Santa Galdana is one of the most popular beaches

This is an excellent place for amateur ornithologists and animal lovers; there are populations of kites and other birds of prey, as well as a profusion of insects including iridescent dragonflies. The cliffs close to Santa Galdana and inland offer an excellent environment for butterflies and are a particularly popular nesting site for migratory swallows that visit in hundreds of thousands each summer.

The rocky coastline on either side of the resort shelter some exquisite beaches that can be reached on foot for a day of walking, swimming and sunbathing on stretches that are less busy than the main resort. About a kilometre to the east is Cala Mitjana, and further east lies Cala Trebalúger. The same distance in the opposite direction, you will find Cala Macarella.

Santa Galdana

Colourful water slides along the beach

Calascoves

One of the wildest and most beautiful calas on the south coast, this narrow curving rocky inlet filled with crystal-clear turquoise water and hiding a tiny pearl of a beach is the yachtsmen's favourite Menorcan anchorage. It can only be reached overland by a 2km-long rough track from Son Vitamina, which saves it from the footfalls of the masses.

Two ravines converge and reach the sea here and the power of the water has sculpted some amazing shapes into the limestone. Numerous pre-Talayotic cave dwellings and a necropolis have been sculpted from the natural caves that were used as a place of pilgrimage until Roman times. Artefacts found during excavations here are on display in the Museum of Menorca in Maó (*see pp42–4*).

The caves became a popular hangout during the hippie era of the 1960s – a paradise for laid-back relaxation that lasted until the late 1990s. Although the 'summer of love' lasted longer here than in many places, it didn't survive into the new millennium. Now the cave-dwellers have been evicted and the site is on the protected list.

Calascoves caves. Open access. Admission free.

Cova des Coloms (Cave of the Pigeons)

Set in the heart of barranca countryside and only reached via a footpath south of Migjorn Gran or northwest from Sant Tomàs, the Cave of the Pigeons is one of the biggest inland caverns on the island. It has been given the nickname 'the Cathedral' for its height and width.

Excavations here have revealed that the cave served as a centre of cult worship for the Talayotic peoples that lived in the surrounding countryside. The cave is now used as an impromptu party venue by local youths or disrespectful backpackers, which accounts for the soot and burn stains around the walls.

Cova des Coloms. By footpath from Estancia Cornabou just south of Es Migjorn Gran. Open access. Admission free.

Crystal clear turquoise waters

The old windmill in Es Mercadal

Es Mercadal

This town forms the crossroads of the island, a junction between roads leading north, south, east and west. It was the natural place to stop for refreshment at a time when travel was undertaken at a more leisurely pace, and it still boasts some excellent restaurants. The proximity of Monte Toro *(see pp111–13)* just a couple of kilometres above the town also made it a natural settling point. Remains from Talayotic and Roman times are evidence that the area has a long history.

The town owes its present status to Jaume II who founded a parish here in the early 1400s. A group of settlers arrived from mainland Spain and the building of Fort Agueda just a few kilometres away guaranteed economic viability.

The licence to hold a market in medieval times gave the town its name. It was the administrative centre for much of the western interior of Menorca until the mid-19th century. It lost control of Es Migjorn Gran as recently as 1989 in an island reshuffle.

Església Sant Martí, built in simple Baroque style and now completely whitewashed, is the dominant building as you approach the town, but the main feature as you drive past on the main road is the old windmill, now converted into a popular restaurant.

The town benefited most directly from the massive *aljub* or public cistern built by Governor Kane in the 18th century to alleviate chronic water shortages. Locals still arrive with pails and other containers to take free water when the gates are open.

Aljub. Open: Sat 10am–1pm. Admission free.

Es Migjorn Gran

Menorca's youngest municipality, Es Migjorn Gran sits a little off the main routes and perhaps it is this that has helped the town retain its cosy, small-town feel. The town was founded in the late 18th century as San Cristóbel but took its new name, meaning 'the big south', when it gained independence from Es Mercadal in the late 1980s.

There is no special attraction that stands out here, though the simple church of Sant Cristòfol straddles the Baroque and Neo-classical styles. The simple domestic architecture and neat, whitewashed family homes are a pleasing sight.

Local hero Francesc Camps I Mercadal (pseudonym Francesc d'Albranca) is remembered for his collections of folkloric tales, songs and dances that have kept Menorcan culture alive. Today his legacy lives on as the town is one of the most active in these traditional arts, contributing musicians and dance troupes to many festival celebrations around the island.

Farinara S'Arangi

You can't miss this large complex set on the side of the main ME-1 between Alaior *(see pp102–3)* and Es Mercadal *(see above)* This old mill is one of a new breed of tourism enterprises – part-museum, part-shopping centre, it offers a stop that caters to the whole family with a small park area for kids plus a bar restaurant.

Huge development has changed the face of Ferreries

Downtown Ferreries

The mill dates from 1905. All the threshing and grinding machinery are still *in situ* and have been restored with great care. The warehouses, with their original wooden floors and ceilings, are now the retail area selling souvenirs that run the whole gamut – though there's more mass-produced stuff than quality handcrafted goods.

Carretera General, Es Mercadal. Tel: 971 15 43 08. Museum open: Tue, Fri & Sat 9am–2pm. Shopping: daily 9am–8pm. Admission charge for museum.

Ferreries

The highest town in Menorca, Ferreries too founded by Jaume II. It is thought that the name derives from the number of blacksmiths that worked here – an ironworks is 'ferreria' in Catalan. Sadly, there is little left of the old town – if you head to the higher part of the town you will see some 18th-century houses. Ferreries has developed into a not-so-attractive inland town because of the huge development in the latter part of the 20th century that focused on the footwear and furniture industries.

Museu de la Natura (Museum of Nature) has a small exhibition devoted to environmental issues but the main reason to visit the town would be its modern main square, Plaça d'Espanya. It hosts a huge open-air market every Friday, and stages numerous folkloric events such as dancing and traditional music concerts, plus craft fairs throughout the summer. Consult the tourist office to get an idea of what is happening here during your stay.
Museu de la Natura. Calle Mallorca 2. Tel: 971 35 07 62. Open: May–Oct

Tue–Sat 10.30am–1.30pm & 5.30–8.30pm; Nov–Apr Tue, Thur & Sat 5.30–8.30pm. Admission charge.

Monte Toro

Menorca's highest point has exerted a strong metaphysical and spiritual influence on the island throughout its known history. Though by no means a true mountain at a height of only 357m, it nonetheless offers spectacular views across the island, and, on early spring or late autumn days, rises above the dewy morning mist that blankets the lowlands.

The access road heads out of Es Mercadal and ends in a series of switchback turns leading to the car park. Here, amidst a rash of modern communications antennas that keep

Monte Toro is the highest point in Menorca

The tombs at Navetes de Rafal Rubi

Menorca in touch with the world, is the holiest site on the island. This is a Christian sanctuary built to house a statue of the Virgin Mary – the Verge del Toro, patron of the island – that is said to be imbued with miraculous powers. A simple Gothic building was initially erected to house the statue, and the Franciscans expanded this into a monastery complex. The place got an ornate Baroque makeover in the 17th century, but was defiled soon after the Franco regime took power in the 1930s, though the statue was saved. She stands holding the infant Jesus and a trusty bull at her feet at the centre of a mock-Baroque altar, the result of repairs carried out in the 1940s. A community of Franciscan nuns now cares for the complex.

Of course this most advantageously situated lookout would not be complete without some kind of fortification and, after the Ottoman raids of 1558, a square watchtower went up. This protected the population and the statue during times of peril, and today is the least altered part of the complex – unfortunately, though, it is off-limits as it is part of an army post.

Crowning the peak is a large statue of 'Jesus' Sacred Heart', depicting Christ with his arms outstretched. The figure sits on an earlier edifice raised to commemorate the Menorcans who fell during wars with the Moroccans in the 1920s; it was added by the then bishop of the island in 1939 after the horror of the Civil War. The mount welcomes a steady stream of pilgrims through the year but truly comes alive during the Festa de la Verge de Toro (Festival of the Virgin of the Bull) on the 8th of May when, after a mass at the church, the congregation heads down the hill for a knees-up at Es Mercadal.

What's in a name?
Menorcans will tell you that the mountain was named Monte Toro because a wild bull (toro) with silver horns led a group of monks to a cave on the peak where they discovered the statue of the Virgin. More probably, the name comes from the Arabic 'al-tor' meaning 'high ground', and the Spanish developed the legend to cover the unpopular original root of the name since it was devised by their old enemies.

Navetes de Rafal Rubi
Twin navetes are rare, so it is good to see these siblings standing in a farmer's field close to the main cross-island road just outside Maó. A well-worn path leads to these communal burial structures resembling upturned boats, one of which is in a better state of preservation than the other. The style and building quality indicate that these belong to the pre-Talayotic era, making them some of the oldest on the island and a contrast to the Naveta des Tudons (*see p132 & p134*), which is much finer in quality and later in date.
ME-1 km 6.6. Open access.
Admission free.

Sant Tomàs
The 3km-long beach at Sant Tomàs (in fact, two beaches Sant Tomàs and Sant

Adeodat, though visitors may not notice the tiny rocky outcrop that separates the two) was undoubtedly the reason for the resort being founded here. But, if you are a novice or non-swimmer, be aware that there are strong undercurrents offshore. The tourist infrastructure is developing fast here and it is a good place for watersports lovers. You also have the opportunity to set off on walks across the southern barrancas: several marked footpaths lead out along the coastline or inland to numerous caves, including the impressive Cova des Coloms (*see p107*) and ancient remains. The best route is probably the one along the Barranc de Binigaus. Here you will find archetypal southern landscapes.

A sign for Navetes de Rafal Rubi

Remains of the paleo-Christian church, Son Bou

Son Bou

The longest beach on the island at 4km, Son Bou is a wide golden stretch that seems to go on forever, and a total contrast to the cosy calas of en Porter (*see pp103–104*) or en Blanes (*see p121*). The duneland backing the fine sand is also unusual in the south. In the centre of the bay, the freshwater reed beds, Es Prat, caused by the natural damming of a river outlet, are the largest of their type in Menorca, and a rich environment for birds, reptiles, butterflies and insects – including mosquitoes.

Son Bou is one of the youngest resorts on the island with a proliferation of low-rise villas and apartment blocks climbing the hillside north of the coastal plain. These are generally in good taste but the same can't be said of the older high-rise Sol Pinguinos Hotel that dominates the bay. Still, Son Bou offers a good range of tourist services, from restaurants and bars to water sports facilities.

The bay at Son Bou also houses some important ancient sites. The remains of the largest paleo-Christian church in Menorca sit on the eastern flank of the beach. The ground plan with its three naves is clearly visible (though not much else). Soon after its discovery in 1951, archaeologists also found traces of a small surrounding settlement, but these haven't been preserved. Behind the church are more ancient carved caves, part of a Talayotic necropolis. A few of these are used as bohemian holiday homes complete with painted shutters and sun terraces.

Be aware that, just as at Sant Tomàs, the sea at Son Bou has strong undercurrents. Look out for the warning flags that warn you of the state of the sea.

Paleo-Christian church. Walled site, free to view.

Son Mercer de Baix

One of the oldest ancient settlements yet excavated on the island, Son Mercer de Baix is quite difficult to get to. So, in many ways, a visit here offers the chance to explore a site without too many 21st-century distractions.

The countryside here is spectacular. Set amongst two verdant barrancas are the remains of several Stone Age houses or house navetes including the Cova d'es Moro (The Moor's Cave). It is not a cave, as the name suggests, but a large house for the aged with a roof

supported by three stone pillars. This single building is now classed as a Menorcan National Monument.
Close to the farm of Son Mercer de Baix 3km south of Ferreries. Reached on foot for the last 600m. Open access. Admission free.

Talayots de Sant Agusti Vell

Close to the Cova des Coloms (*see p107*) is the early ancient site of Sant Agusti Vell, set at the peak of a typical barranca. There are the remains of several houses and a collection of sitjots or storage chambers that have been carved out of rock. When in use these would have been covered with stone slabs.

The finest remains on the site are two high talayots, one of which has a chamber that you can climb into. The main interior structures are the two stone pillars supporting the upper structure. The village was inhabited from the pre-Talayotic to the Roman era, and finds include artefacts of Phoenician origin.
Access on foot from the ME-18 Es Migjorn Gran to Sant Tomàs road. Open access (the route is not good). Admission free.

Torre d'en Gaumés

The largest Talayotic town in Menorca, Torre d'en Gaumés sits on a hill with long-distance views in all directions, as far as Mallorca on a good day. The lower part of the settlement comprises numerous stone homes; many still

Son Bou beach is the longest on the island

A cove on the southern coast

exhibit their impressive pillars, though the stone roofs they supported are no longer set atop them. Around them are a handful of sitjots carved into the base rock.

Climbing up through the village, more unexcavated buildings come into view. The village has three talayots and a taula set within its enclosure – the ceremonial slab has fallen from its support, however.

The settlement finds cover the same eras as the Sant Agusti Vell site (*see p115*) but archaeologists also found medieval remains, suggesting that a part of the site was occupied well after this time, though it no longer functioned as a village. The finest piece discovered is surely the ancient Egyptian brass statue of Imhotep now on display in the Museum of Menorca (*see pp42–4*) at Maó.

The necropolis site of Ses Roques Llises lies 300m beyond the village. Dating back to the pre-Talayotic period, it comprises a rectangular chamber lined with large flagstones and, close to this, a large ancient structure of five chambers and a walled patio with the separate name of Na Comerma de sa Garita. *Signposted off the Son Bou road. Open access. Admission free.*

Torralba d'en Salord

One of the most easily comprehensible of the island's many ancient sites, Torralba d'en Salord has been thoroughly excavated since the 1970s, and is the village that has added most to the growing academic understanding of pre-Talayotic and Talayotic cultures in Menorca. The site is made up of several houses inhabited throughout pre-history, a central talayot, the tallest taula on the island, a quarry, threshing area and sections of a cyclopean outer wall – suggesting that some of the sites were protected by fortifications. At some time during the intervening centuries the site used to be cut by a country lane but the route has now been diverted around the site.

C14 tests on various areas show that the site was established c1400 BC with the Talayotic houses dating from c1300 BC. When the taula area was excavated archaeologists discovered many cult items including terracotta figures of a Punic deity, and a small ceremonial bronze bull that links these ancient people with other bull-worshipping cults around the Mediterranean basin. These finds were all dated to the 2nd and 1st centuries BC, and are on display in the Museum of Menorca (*see pp42–4*) in Maó.

More mundane items were discovered in the houses: the bones of numerous ovicaprids (ancient forms of sheep and goat), and wheat and barley seeds that indicated the inhabitants' regular diet.

There are no navetes at the Torralba d'en Salord site but it does include a series of funerary hypogeums or artificial caves to contain bodies, carved in the rock.

4km east of Alaior on the Cala'n Porter road. Open: Jun–Sept daily 10am–8pm; Oct–May Mon–Sat 10am–1pm & 3–6pm. Admission charge.

Torralba d'en Salord

In 1985, Menorcan cheese makers applied for and were granted a 'denomination of origin' mark – which means that only cheese produced on the island under the strict guidelines of the regulatory authority may be given the label 'Mahón-Menorca'. Each Denominación de Origen Protegida (D.O.P.) cheese will have been quality-checked and will have a numbered label. This protects the quality of the product and allows you to recognise it in shops or factories.

Before the advent of modern technology cheese would have been made at the farm or *lloc* by the farmer who would have overseen the curing process in one of his barns. This involved turning the cheese regularly and rubbing the rind with a blend of oils and spices – each farm had its own secret recipe – that would impart a particular flavour. Today, many of the cheeses are made in factories but quality is still paramount.

One of the staples of the farming industry, Menorcan cheese or queso has developed into an art object. The Moors sang its praises and Menorcans were exporting it across the Mediterranean as early as the 13th century.

CONSELL REGULADOR DE LA DE NOMINACIÓ D' ORIGEN
MAHÓN · MENORCA

mahón
MENORCA

WHAT TO TASTE
Today's product is made and air-cured or matured following long-established

Cheese has long been a speciality of Menorca and there are a wide variety available

traditions, from fine-quality cow's milk. It is sold in three main categories.

Young

These are cheeses that have been matured for between 21 and 60 days. The product has a soft, supple and elastic texture, and a pale yellow colour. The flavour is just a little sharp.

Semi-cured

As the cheese matures further it takes on a lighter colour with a brownish or orange and slightly wrinkled rind, and a firmer texture. It now has a characteristic smell and a tangier flavour. A cheese is classed as semi-cured when it is between two and five months old.

Cured

With even further maturing the cheese hardens, the texture becomes more brittle and crumbly, and the taste stronger. It is classed as 'cured' when it has been maturing for over five months.

Aged

With a rind that resembles old leather and flesh the colour of parchment, these are cheeses that have matured for well over a year or longer. The flavour has strength and complexity, and a long aftertaste. It is excellent when accompanied by a fortified wine.

NAMES TO LOOK FOR

The following brands have been recognised by the Menorcan cheese council (*for more details consult www.quesomahonmenorca.com in Spanish only*): Binibeca, Coinga, Dalrit, H. De FCO Quintana, Hort de Sant Patrici, Marqués, Mercadal, La Payesa, Sa Casanova, Subaida and Torralba.

WHERE TO TRY IT

You can taste Menorcan cheese at market stalls or vendors or try it in one of the island's recipes: in a delicious four-cheese soup with some of each style incorporated into the recipe, or in cheese ice cream – which tastes much better than it sounds – served crème brulée-style with a crispy sweet coating.

The town of Alaior (*see p102–103*) is a centre of commercial cheese production with two factories – the Coinga (c/d'Es Mercadal) and the La Payesa (c/d'Es Banyer 64).

Western Menorca

The sunset coast of Menorca is anchored by Ciutadella, the city of sandstone mansions, the religious heart of the island and its prettiest port. The old town is most enjoyable at any time of day but a warm glow becomes palpable as evening descends and the streets come alive after the long afternoon siesta.

Boutique on the Quadrado

Just a couple of kilometres north of the town is the island's largest tourist agglomeration – three picture-perfect calas, now known as Cala en Forcat, that have grown into a small town full of budget hotels, apartment blocks and eateries. In the evenings it is a good place for genuine fish and chips and a pint of Guinness.

Cala'n Bosc to the south has more sand and fewer hotels, plus a marina that is the perfect spot for a tourist-dominated paseo and a waterfront dinner.

These two resorts offer over 90% of the accommodation in the west but it is easy to escape the crowds by going to the calas of the west, called *platjes verges* or virgin beaches by the Menorcans for their unspoilt natural beauty. Cala en Turqueta east of Cala'n Bosc is considered the most beautiful on the island, but there are many more whose golden sands and azure waters backed by limestone cliffs are just waiting to be discovered if you have your own transport.

The landscape around Ciutadella epitomises the contrast between the migjorn and the tramuntana. To the south you will find date palms and neat citrus groves, while to the north the eye sees nothing but arid desert with kilometres of dry-stone walls, hundreds of barraques and rare farmhouses.

Cala d'Algaiarens

Lying east of Cala Morell, the twin beaches of d'Algaiarens are two of the north coast's most exquisite horseshoe bays of fine golden sand, backed by tall pines. They are impossible to reach by

A small hotel in Cala'n Bosc

public transport and the landowner limits the number of cars travelling across his land to the bays. The trip makes for a great cycle ride and the quiet beaches are certainly worth it. *Intersection of the Cala Morell road. 3.5km to the beach. Access charge for vehicles.*

Cala'n Bosc (also Cala en Bosc and pronounced 'cala n bosh')

Cala'n Bosc successfully combines beach resort with lively marina, and is one of Menorca's enduring favourites. The town beach is pretty but small. The wider Platja Son Xoriguer is within walking distance to the east and has been incorporated into the growing resort area. The marina is a lovely place for an evening stroll, lined with restaurants and bars. You can take a day trip from here or rent boats, and head out to explore the coast.

For sheer holiday facilities, head inland to the outskirts of the town where you will find Aquarock with huge pools, slides, jacuzzi and a children's play area. Aquarock is an alternative to the sticky sand and salty water of the beach, and KartingRock is a karting venue with single or double karts.
Aquarock: Off Via de Circumval Lagó Tel: 971 38 78 22.
Open: daily 10.30am–6pm.
KartingRock: Off Via de Circumval Lagó Tel: 971 38 78 22.
Open: 10.30am–10.30pm.
Kart charges.

Cala en Forcat

Several tourist developments have come up along the coast a couple of kilometres north of Ciutadella, around a series of picturesque narrow calas. The once individual resorts of Cala en Forcat, Cala en Blanes and Los Delphines have fused to create the island's largest holiday complex and in high season the little coves are filled by visitors. There is nothing sophisticated here, just pure family fun with big-screen matches in the football season accompanied by an English or German pint.

The resort boasts a water park that has slides, chutes, freshwater pools and a café/bar. The large hotel and apartment complexes have discos in peak season for night owls.
Aqua Center: Avenida Principal, Cala en Blanes.
Tel: 971 38 82 51. www.aquacenter-menorca.com.
Open: May–Oct daily 10.30am–6.30pm. Admission charge.

Western Menorca

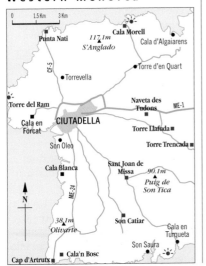

Cala Morell

Cala Morell has a stark and alluring beauty. A barren rocky inlet sheltering a postage stamp-sized golden beach, it makes an incredible anchorage for yachters. The only vegetation around are hundreds of cultivated palms and colourful bougainvillea, softening the lines of the upmarket whitewashed villas that tumble down the cliffs towards the waterline. The panorama is one of the most dramatic in Menorca.

Cala Morell is an artificial oasis in one of the least populated parts of the island (*see Getting Away From it All p146*) and one could be forgiven for thinking that only modern man has the wherewithal to survive here. In fact, however, the cliffs around the resort have one of the highest densities of rock-cut ancient caves in Europe and around 1000 BC the bay was buzzing with the activities of the Talayotic people.

Explore the caves of Cala Morell

Cala Morell

The Cuevas de Cala Morell bring home the sophistication of these people. Expansive chambers interlink to create the interiors of a modern studio apartment with carved wall niches and even windows. Some of the openings sport carved detail that must have obviously taken a great deal of time and patience to accomplish. There are over 15 caves in total, some used as dwellings, and others as storage areas and ossuaries. The caves were in use from pre-Talayotic times to the end of the Roman era.

On the approach to town, look out for the Torre d'en Quart, a sturdy medieval tower built to protect against pirate attack and now incorporated into a typical *lloc* complex.

Cuevas de Cala Morell. Open access. Admission charge.

Cap d'Artrutx

Menorca's southwesternmost corner is a rugged, rocky spot marked by a mid-19th-century lighthouse that was an important guide for ships. There are incredible sunsets here and clear views of the island of Mallorca less than 40km away.

The tower close by, Talaia d'Artrutx, dates from 1588 and was one of a series built in the wake of violent Ottoman attacks. A string of towers around the coast acted as an early warning system. In times of danger a warning fire would be lit at one tower that could be seen by the next tower down the coast, which would in turn light a fire, and so on, until the whole island was on alert.

A street in Cala en Forcat

Cala Morell bay

Ciutadella

Menorca's old capital is its most beautiful city. When the British took executive power away from Ciutadella they inadvertently did its citizens a favour, preserving the patrician palazzi and religious institutions for posterity. Once a walled citadel, the town is a compact district with tree-lined avenues of 'contramadura'. The port is the perfect place for an evening aperitif and alfresco dinner.

Founded by the Carthaginians, the town was the only major settlement on the island at the time of the Moorish takeover (some theologians contend that it was already a Bishopric), and was the natural site for their capital, 'Medina Minurka', which sat on the site of the Cathedral square. The town was given the name Ciutadella when the Christians retook the island. It remained the capital with power concentrated in the hands of a few influential families even when sovereignty passed through the hands of many other European powers.

In 1558 the city was destroyed by Ottoman forces, allied with France against Charles V. Well over half of the population was forcibly taken to Istanbul to be sold in the slave markets. Only a hefty ransom paid by the remaining islanders could secure their release.

The city was reinforced in the wake of the attacks but it didn't make it any more enticing to the British who really only coveted the harbour at Maó. When the islands finally became and remained Spanish, Maó was proclaimed capital

Ottoman Memorial in the main square

Ciutadella harbour

but the diocese stayed at Ciutadella – and the patrician families stayed put in the town.

With the growing population bursting through the city walls, they were demolished in 1860. In the following decades the city thrived as a centre of the shoe industry. It suffered during the Spanish Civil War in 1936 after the garrison declared loyalty to Franco while the rest of the island remained staunchly for the Republic. Many of the churches were ransacked in violent retribution.

Today, the city is a wonderful throwback to a bygone era with fine architecture at every corner. Although we have listed the major attractions here, wandering through the narrow streets is the best way to appreciate the grace and beauty of the whole.

Bastió de Sa Font and the Museu Municipal (Ciutadella Municipal Museum)

The only remaining element of a 17th-century city wall, Bastió de Sa Font stands strong and proud at the head of the Ciutadella inlet. After it lost its strategic value as a fortification, it became a factory producing acetylene gas for street lighting and then was part of the municipal waterworks before being renovated for use as the town museum.

The expansive lower vaults display an interesting collection of artefacts from ancient sites in the western part of the island including excavated skeletons and ritual objects. They also house models of several megalithic settlements.

Plaça Sa Font. Tel: 971 38 02 97.
Open: Tue–Sat 10am–2pm.
Admission charge.

Cathedral de Santa Maria

Before the Moorish takeover of the island, an 8th-century parish church of Santa Maria stood on this spot.

The present building was founded on the site of the main mosque of the Medina Minurka (the bell tower is part of the Islamic complex) in the first days after Alphonso III retook the islands in 1287. This basic Gothic core with its vast single nave still sits at the heart of today's cathedral.

Badly damaged in the attacks of 1558, the flying buttresses were reinforced against possible further attack, giving the exterior the peculiar box shape it has today. It was renovated in the style of the day with the addition of several Baroque side chapels, the finest of which is La Capilla de las Animas (Chapel of the Souls).

The original 14th-century entranceway, the Port de la Llum, is still *in situ* with the coats of arms of Aragon and of the city incorporated into the decoration. Today's main door – a grand portico – on the western façade was part of an early 19th-century makeover that was started soon after the church was elevated to the status of a cathedral in 1795.

Plaça Sa Cathedral. Open: daily 9am–1pm & 6–9pm.

Es Port (The Waterfront)

The port sits in the shadow of the town, much like at Maó, but the narrow cala at Ciutadella gives it a much cosier feel than the waterfront in the capital. It is lined with old whitewashed cottages now housing restaurants and bars, and yachts and tour boats bob at the quayside just a couple of metres away. It is a great place to stroll and is particularly atmospheric in the evenings. You can reach the port via a wide set of steps – the biaxada de Capllonc – that are filled with stalls selling crafts and souvenirs in the late afternoon, or the Moll del Costa that weaves its way behind the Ajuntament. From the north bank of the cala there are good views back across the port and up to the town above.

Head up the creek inland to the Pla la de Sant Joan where the cliffs house ancient caves and warehouses, many

Cathedral de Santa Maria

The harbour front is lined with restaurants and bars

now converted into restaurants and nightclubs. The upper terraces offer some of the best views of the Festa de Sant Joan (*see p26 & p133*) when jousting contests and feats of horsemanship are held here on 23rd and 24th June.

Església del Roser (Roser Church)

The finest example of Churrigueresque architecture (*see p25*) in Menorca, this tiny church was built at the beginning of the 18th century and is little altered from the original. The exterior decoration reveals a wealth of ornate tracery. Now deconsecrated, the interior hosts exhibitions of contemporary art.

c/del Roser. Open: Mon–Sat 10am–1pm & 5–8pm. Admission free.

Mercat (Market)

The meat and charcuterie market with neat tiled stalls was created in 1868 by adapting the cloisters of the Augustinian monastery complex behind it. A separate 19th-century pavilion houses a small fish market. This is a characterful and bustling district where locals gather for a gossip and coffee before heading home for lunch.

Plaça de la Llibertat.
Open: Tue–Sat 8am–1pm.

Museu Diocesa
(Diocesan Museum of Menorca)

Hidden behind another monolithic Baroque façade are the remains of the the 17th-century convent of Saint Augustine which now host the Diocese

Mercat

Museum. As with the Museum of Menorca (*see p42–4*), the architectural elements of this building are as interesting as the museum artefacts. The Mediterranean-style Baroque cloisters make a fine statement.

The galleries have some surprising inclusions, such as an archaeological gallery that has the personal collection of Bishop Mercader including bronze statues dating from the 5th century BC. Another exhibits paintings by the 20th-century Menorcan artist Pere Daura who was known for his landscapes. The more expected objects include an array of liturgical and religious artefacts including several in gold and silver, dating from the 17th to the 20th centuries.

The convent church of the Socors is now a concert venue.

c/Seminari 7. Tel: 971 48 12 97.
Open: Tue–Sat 10.30am–1.30pm.
Admission charge.

Ses Voltes (The Arches)

At one section of the main shopping alleyway running through the Plaça de la Cathedral to meet up with the start of the road to Maó are Ses Voltes, two sets of Gothic-style buildings. They have vaulted porticos with homes above and shops set underneath the arches at ground level. This area is one of the most atmospheric areas in the town.

S'Hostal

The sandstone of the migjorn has been used as building material for millennia. Its warm hue enhances the Talayotic, Gothic, Baroque and Modernist buildings across the island. Its structure made it easy to carve, giving us the fine carved portals of churches such as Santa Eulalia at Alaior (see p103 & p136) and the Cathedral at Ciutadella (see p126). There are working quarries of sandstone across the island even now but most of the old ones have been abandoned or put to use as communal rubbish dumps; making them a detraction from the landscape rather than an element in Menorca's socio-economic heritage.

Lithica changed all that. This non-profit organisation aims to rehabilitate the sites of the old quarries, and to educate Menorcans and visitors about the important role played by these 'holes in the ground'.

The quarry workings at Ciutadella were worked for over 200 years before they were closed in 1994. The cuttings demonstrate two different means of extraction – the 19th-century hammer and chisel approach leaving a maze of block-work towers and indents behind, and the 20th-century method involving huge circular saws that could cut deeper vertically into the stone leaving vast clean faces behind.

At S'Hostal the complex has been planted with native and tropical plants. Olives, oranges and almonds offer shade, and there are several water features to enjoy. It is a wonderful place to wander around with interesting views down into the complex and from the quarry base. A whole host of butterflies, insects and birds now call it home.

The cathedral-like dimensions of the

Tourists in Ciutadella

S'Hostall Quarry is sometimes used as a venue for concerts

Steps in the S'Hostal quarry

20th-century quarry are now put to good use as it doubles as a concert venue on summer evenings.
Cami Vell (1km east of town).
Tel: 971 48 15 78 www.lithica.com.
Open: daily 9.30am–sunset.
Admission charge.

Plaça d'es Born

The finest town square in Menorca, Plaça d'es Born is a wide open space, home to trees, cafés and the town's bi-weekly market (*Fri & Sat am*). From the northern flank there is a viewing point –

More Information
The tourist office at Ciutadella is at Plaça de Sa Cathedral (in the Cathedral square).
Tel: 971 38 26 93. www.e-menorca.org

the mirador – down to the port below but this is the smallest of Born's treasures. Menorca's natural sandstone has been used to exceptional effect here to erect several impressive buildings around the periphery. The overall effect is that these have been here for centuries but in fact they are mostly 19th-century. At the heart of the square is an obelisk commemorating the attack of 1558 and the bravery of the people.

The eye-catching Ajuntament (once the Town Hall, now the Police Headquarters) has traces of old Moorish architecture with its arches and fringe of date palms. The building sits on the site of a Roman temple. Teatre des Born on the northern façade was built on the site of the old British barracks building in 1873, and is now the centre for the arts in western Menorca.

On the eastern flank are two exceptional 19th-century palaces that together form an architectural whole. Both have impressive Neo-classical façades featuring three-arched loggias on the first floor. The Torresaura Palace is the larger of the two with twin towers linked by a single-storey entrance topped by an ornate family coat of arms. Next door is Palace Salort, set at an angle to the square, its main façade overlooking c/Major des Borns. Both palaces are still in private hands but the Palau de Salort

A bead of hope
A vision of tortured realism, the crucifixion in the high Baroque Capella del Sant Christ has been an object of devotion for many generations. It is said that in 1661 sweat appeared on the brow of Christ, and parishioners still believe that this statue can help alleviate human suffering.

The Ajuntament, now the Police Headquarters

is open to the public during restricted hours. You can enjoy the period interior décor and furniture here.

Església Sant Francesc at the southwestern corner was once part of a larger convent complex. It was destroyed in the 1558 attack, and restored and augmented in the following centuries. The façade was the final addition in the 19th century.
Palau de Salort.
Open: May–Oct Mon–Sat 10am–2pm.
Admission charge.

The mouth of the inlet

The mouth of the Ciutadella inlet is a pleasant walk of around a kilometre from the port. The narrow and rocky channel makes it clear why the Royal Navy wouldn't have wanted to run a base from here. The regular ferry between here and Mallorca seems to manage pretty well, though, and it is fun to watch its immense bulk sliding between the inlet's walls, reminiscent of tankers traversing the Suez Canal.

On the north side of the inlet is the lighthouse of Punta na Mari; and on the south is the small but perfectly formed Castell de Sant Nicolau built at the end of the 16th century to defend the port and town. The tower was restored in the 1980s.
Castell de Sant Nicolau.
Plaça Admiral Farragut.
Tel: 971 38 10 50. Open:
Tue–Sun 11am–1pm &
6-8pm. Admission free.

Naveta des Tudons

The finest single ancient building in Menorca and one of the finest ancient ossuaries in Europe (claims have also been made that it is the oldest roofed building in the continent), the Naveta des Tudons marks a high point in the building techniques and burial rituals of the pre-Talayotic/Talayotic peoples. During earlier phases, the bones of the dead were interred in caves or carved hypogeums. The naveta represented a sophisticated development, a custom-built and monolithic tomb where ancestors and their treasured possessions could rest in peace.

In use between 1200 and 750 BC, the Naveta des Tudons was a large (14m x 6m) communal tomb with two internal chambers. It was fully excavated in the 1950s when the remains of

A MENORCAN IN AMERICA

David Glasgow Farragut was the son of a Ciutadellan who had emigrated to the United States. He fought in the Civil War and was head of the force that took New Orleans. Eventually he reached the rank of Admiral – the first in the American Navy. When he visited Ciutadella in 1867 he was welcomed as a celebrity and it is said that the crowd was so dense that Farragut's carriage couldn't finish its journey and he had to walk the final section, with well-wishers tugging at his person.

There's a bust dedicated to Farragut in the square in front of Castell Sant Nicolau.

Festa de Sant Joan

The Festival of St John is Menorca's most important religious and cultural celebration. The two-day festivities were begun in the 14th century as a show of prestige by the city's patrician families. Over the centuries, it developed into a display of horsemanship. Even in the present day every two years, responsibility for organisation of the celebration is passed from one family to another. The year's 'Caixer Senyor' manages the show and its complicated rituals.

The Sunday before the 24th, S'Homo d'es Bé (man of the Lamb), a representation of John the Baptist clad in fleece and carrying a lamb, is paraded through the town by a party of horsemen.

On the 23rd, a cavalcade starts the festivities at 2pm to the accompaniment of the jaleo (traditional music played on a flute) and a host of medieval flags and costumes. The black horses or 'bot', on their hind legs with front legs high in the air, trot around Plaça d'es Born – this is Menorcan dressage at its very best. At 7.30pm there is a mass at Sant Joan de Missa (see p134) in the countryside outside the town.

On the morning of the 24th there are jousting trials in the Plaça Sant Joan (open ground at the head of the Ciutadella inlet), and then a mass at the cathedral. At 6pm the master of the festa is invited to come and watch the climax of the jousts when only the most skilled horsemen appear. When the victors are declared there is a final cavalcade that wends its way to the church of Santa Clara. A spectacular fireworks display ends the day.

Cruise boats line the waterfront on the marina

Naveta des Tudons is one of the finest ossuaries in Europe

over 100 individuals were found with grave goods including bronze bracelets, bone buttons and clay pots.

40km on the ME-1 (5km east of Ciutadella). Open access. Admission free.

Punta Nati

The lighthouse at Punta Nati *(see p99)* – known as Farola Nova – was built at the beginning of the 20th century with money donated by the French after one of their cross-Mediterranean passenger ships ran aground on the rocks killing or injuring over 200 people. There are several walking trails along the coastline from here and it offers exceptional sunset views.

This route makes for a great cycling trip from Ciutadella or from the Cala en Forcat resorts because it is mostly flat land; you will need to carry your own refreshments, though.

Sant Joan de Missa

Founded in the first days after the re-establishment of Christianity on the island at the end of the 13th century, the original Gothic *ermita* has undergone many extensions and renovations including battlements added in the 1630s – the whitewash does a fair job in bringing the disparate elements into a coherent whole.

The chapel, also known locally as Sant Joan Gran, is the centre of attention during the Festa de Sant Joan *(see p133)* when a colourful procession wends its way from Ciutadella to attend mass.

4km southeast of Ciutadella. Not open regular hours. Admission free.

Torre Llafuda

The talayot of this ancient village is believed to be the largest in Menorca. A small taula and a cave plus short sections of a cyclopean wall and stone passageways are still visible. The settlement was one of the most important in the region during Roman times and was inhabited until the end of the Moorish era.

Just off the ME-1 at km 37.
Open access. Admission free.

Torre Trencada

This ancient site has yet to be fully excavated and contrasts with the village at Torralba d'en Salord (*see pp116–17*) which is well signposted and mapped. Those who enjoy history will love it here, clambering amongst the remains of ancient stone houses. The main attraction at Torre Trencada is the taula. This is thought to be still in its original configuration, as the ancients intended, though the enclosure has been lost. The site is thought to have been inhabited until the Middle Ages.

7km east of Ciutadella on the Cami Vell (Maó to Ciutadella old road).
Open access. Admission free.

Within these walls

The prehistoric site at Son Catlar in the countryside southeast of Ciutadella is the only one to have retained its immense defensive wall. It extends for almost a kilometre and, within the compound, you will be able to explore five talayots and other scattered remains.
8km southeast of Ciutadella. Open: 10am–sunset. Admission charge in summer.

The lighthouse in Punta Nati was built in the beginning of the last century

Drive: Across the Spine of Menorca

Menorca is a compact island and you can easily get from east to west in a day. The main ME-1 links several interesting towns and villages that offer a contrast to the beach resorts around the coast. The drive finishes at Ciutadella where you can take a drink on the port side.

Distance: 56km.

Time: 6 hours.

Leave Maó by travelling west along the waterfront until you reach a roundabout. Take route ME-7 signposted Fornells. After 2.5km turn left on the Cami d'en Kane.

1 Cami d'en Kane

The Cami d'en Kane was the first cross-island road built under the auspices of Richard Kane, the first British Governor of Menorca, in the early 1800s. The route is narrow and winding with high stone walls leading through some wonderful rolling countryside.

Follow Cami d'en Kane until you reach the outskirts of Alaior after 10km. There is a turn left at the town cemetery, which leads into the town.

2 Alaior

Alaior is famous for its cheese and on a warm summer's day there is a faint whiff in the air around town. Visit the factories to buy supplies and stroll in the lanes of the old town. The Church of Santa Eulalia has a fine Baroque façade.

From Alaior pick up the main ME-1 route by following directions for Ciutadella (this main route bypasses the town to the south but is well signposted from the centre). Continue west until you reach the Farinara S'Arangí on the right after 7km.

3 Farinara S'Arangí

This old mill complex was built in 1905 and remained in operation until 1999. Today, it is a museum complex, shopping mall and restaurant – there is even a small park for children.

From the mill complex continue west for 1km. On the outskirts of Es Mercadal follow signs right for Monte Toro and climb the winding lane to the summit.

4 Monte Toro

Monte Toro is Menorca's highest point and there are almost 360° views from the peak. The huge statue of Christ was added in the years after the civil war in the late 1930s but there has been a church on the site for several hundred years earlier. This is the home of the statue of the Virgin with the Bull, the

patron saint of the island.
Descend the hill again and make your way to Es Mercadal.

5 Es Mercadal

Founded in the 14th century, Es Mercadal is home to the Església Sant Martí. A vast communal *aljub* or water cistern was built during Kane's governorship.
Return to the ME-1 and continue west on to Ferreries, reached after 8km.

6 Ferreries

Ferreries is a centre of folkloric music and dance. Performances take place throughout the summer at the Plaça d'Espanya.
Continue west. After 39km look for a small cottage on the right-hand side of the road. This is one of three 'Peones Camineros' left on the island – they were free accommodation for the foremen in charge of keeping the roads of Menorca in working order. A little further on, look for signs to the left leading to the car park for the Naveta des Tudons.

7 Naveta des Tudons

One of the finest ancient monuments in Europe, the Naveta des Tudons is situated 300m away. You can climb inside to take a look at the ossuary chamber.
From the naveta, it is only 4km to your destination, the city of Ciutadella.

8 Ciutadella

The attractions at Ciutadella can fill a whole day but on this itinerary you will have time only to get a feel of the place while strolling through the streets and along the waterfront.

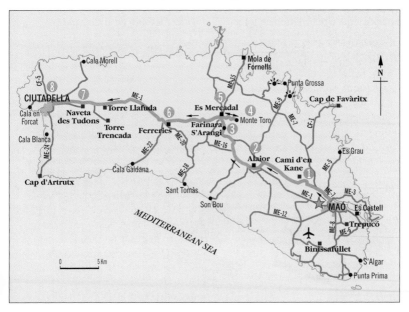

Walk: The Sights of Ciutadella

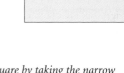

Much of the old district of Ciutadella is off-limits to traffic so it is very pleasant to stroll around. This route is short but packed with attractions.

Time: 2½ hours.

Distance: 2.5km.

Start at the Plaça d'es Born. If you have arrived by car the square offers ample parking except on market days (Fri and Sat am).

1 Plaça d'es Born

Stroll around the Plaça d'es Born enjoying the façades of the 19th-century palaces and the Ajuntament with its Moorish details. The obelisk at the heart of the square commemorates the 1558 attack on the city by Ottoman forces.

Leave the square by taking the narrow lane Major dei Borne that leads between the two palaces on the eastern side.

2 Major dei Borne

The buildings of the Major dei Borne have a timeless quality with elements of the palazzi on the upper floors. The lower vaulted storeys now house shops selling souvenirs and Menorcan foodstuffs.

After a couple of hundred metres, you will enter the Plaça de la Catedral.

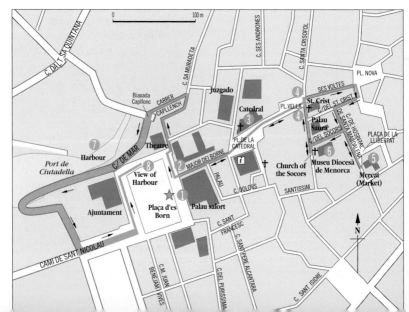

3 Catedral de Santa Maria

The city tourist office is on the right and on the left is the Catedral de Santa Maria with its Gothic core embellished by Baroque and 19th-century additions. Visit the Chapel of the Souls in the interior and study the details of the original medieval entrance portal on the south side of the building.

Leave the square with the cathedral on your left, opposite where you entered. On your immediate right you will find the first section of the shopping arcades of Ses Voltes.

4 Ses Voltes

A wonderfully cool place to escape the heat of the late morning, Ses Voltes runs for around 300m through two sections. The vaults house a range of shops from tacky souvenir emporia to high-class boutiques.

At the intersection of Ses Voltes with Plaça Nova, turn right and right again into c/ del Sant Crist. Then turn left into c/ de 'Hospital de Santa Magdalena and walk straight ahead into Plaça de la Llibertat.

5 Mercat (Market)

Ciutadella's atmospheric daily food market is situated here with a row of tiled kiosks selling fresh and preserved vegetables, and a separate glass and iron building for fresh fish. It is busiest in the mornings when everyone is out shopping for the evening's meal.

From the market retrace your steps for 100m or so then turn left down c/ del Socors. At the next intersection turn left. Immediately on the left is the Church of the Socors and beyond that the entrance to the Diocese Museum.

6 Museu Diocesà de Menorca

The convent is an excellent example of Baroque architecture and the liturgical and archaeological displays have some interesting pieces.

From the museum turn right to Ses Voltes. Turn left here and retrace your route back to Place d'es Born. Turn right and exit the square by the narrow lane to the right of the theatre. Follow the road around until you reach the Biaxada Capllonc steps. Take the steps down to the port.

7 Harbour

Enjoy strolling past the yachts moored at the quayside and perhaps stop for a drink. The north side of the inlet offers excellent views back across the town, the sheer rock face and buildings above.

Leave the port via c/ de Mar; the curved lane leads back to Plaça d'es Born. Turn left and walk past the Town Hall for an overview.

8 View of the harbour from Plaça d'es Born

This is the best spot to look down on the port where you have just been strolling.

Farmers market in Ciutadella

Getting Away From It All

Menorca is a small island that is packed with tourists in summer but it is still amazingly easy to leave the crowds behind. A maze of dirt tracks that complement the network of smooth, asphalted roads leads to secret coves, whitewashed *llocs*, remote ancient sites and windswept cliffs and promontories. You may even find a castle as you move around.

A dirt track

The island offers even greater rewards to those who are comfortable on bicycles or with donning shoes for walking. From this perspective you will be able to really appreciate the small details – like lichens on the stone walls or tiny flowers growing close to the ground on rocky outcrops. You will also be able to take in the birdsong and the distant music of sheep bells. You will find herds of sheep massed in the scant shade of oleaster and holm oak trees, especially during hot and dry summer days.

Cap de Cavalleria

The Cap de Cavalleria is Menorca's northernmost point, a narrow finger of land that lies far away from the busy resorts. Located to the west of Fornells, it can be reached by a minor though perfectly good road that leads through arid landscapes with rocky bays, such as the Cova des Vell Mari, where there are few sandy stretches.

Although it looks barren, this part of the island was well populated in ancient times and is extremely rich in archaeological remains – so much so that it has been declared an 'area of special interest' by the authorities. The Romans built a city at Sanjita, the sheltered inlet on the western flank that is now being excavated. The exciting discoveries here are revealing the rich culture of the cape in the early first millennium. The ongoing work should give us much more information in the decade to come.

EXCURSIÓN EN BARCO
BOAT TRIP

INFORMACIÓN Y RESERVAS AQUÍ
INFORMATION AND BOOKINGS HERE

Excited passengers board a boat for an excursion

The inlet has a tiny port that is a popular yachting anchorage in summer, and home to just a scatter of tiny fishing boats out of season. On the western tip there is a ruined Martello tower built by the British in 1798.

At the tip of the cape, reached through a couple of gates (close them after you have gone through), sits the oldest lighthouse on the island. It has had a recent facelift with a couple of coats of paint. There are some surprising cliffscapes pounded by the Mediterranean with caves that were carved during the Spanish Civil War.

The farm at Cavalleria, 4km south of the lighthouse, has opened an ecomuseum with finds from the site plus information about the surrounding environment.

At the base of the cape to the west is Platja de Cavalleria, the best in this area

A sign for the ecomuseum at Cavalleria

and a good place to cool off after your exploration. Better beaches lie further west (*see p146*).

Ecomuseu Cavalleria, Finca de Sa Cavalleria. Tel: 971 35 99 99. Open: Jul–Sept daily 10am–8.30pm, Apr–Jun & Oct 10am–7pm. Admission charge.

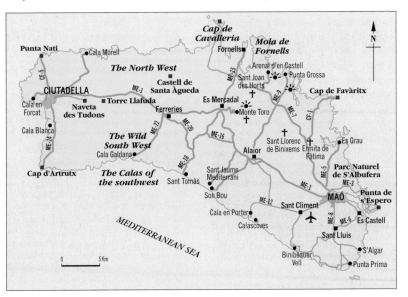

The lighthouse at Cap de Cavalleria is the oldest in Menorca

Mola de Fornells

To the east of Fornells (*see pp88–91*) and its bay, the Badia de Fornells (*see pp85–6*), is the peninsula of Mola de Fornells. This area offers one of the easiest ways to enjoy 'Getting Away From It All' without heading too far from a good bar and restaurant.

Most of the cape is easy walking country lying less than 40m above sea level. The vegetation is mostly low-growing here (since the tramuntana sweeps across the land throughout the winter), so you can get excellent views over the landscape and across to Fornells west across the bay. The highest point on the peninsula, on the eastern flank of the mouth of the narrow inlet, rises to 122m. It affords breathtaking views west to the windswept grey slate of the Cap de Favàritx and, behind that, the Cap de Cavalleria.

The footpaths lead to several coastal caves along the eastern flank, including the immense Cova dels Anglesos (Cave of the English), a huge cathedral-like space that can also be reached by a boat trip from Fornells in the summer.

Foners

In Roman times the Balearic Islands were noted for their foners or slingshot throwers who could launch single rocks or any other projectile with great accuracy and force over long distances. Foners were considered the snipers of their day and were often sent in at the start of a battle to shock and disorient the enemy. Many of them were mercenaries who would sell their services to the highest bidder. Others made a career in the Roman army and travelled across the empire from the Levant to the British Isles.

On the southeastern flank of the peninsula is Arenal de s'Offa, an excellent beach that will soon be incorporated into the Son Parc (*see pp94–5*) resort, while the inlet of Cala Roja at the head of the Badia de Fornells is a pleasant little sandy cove.

Punta Nati

The route to Punta Nati is one of a decreasing number of traditional Menorcan country lanes. Flanked by high dry-stone walls and only one-and-a-half cars wide, it cuts across the arid plains northeast of Ciutadella. Sections of it have recently been upgraded to allow for easier access, particularly for cycles.

The area is extraordinarily beautiful; the almost sepia-tone landscape of sand-

The lighthouse at Punta Nati

The route to Punta Nati

A couple get away from the crowds to enjoy the picturesque view

coloured rocks and golden dry grasses is alleviated only by the thousands of sheep (if you can't see them you can hear the constant jingling of the bells round their necks) and scores of stone sheep pens or barraques that rise tens of metres above the ground. These are incredible feats of engineering for their simple task (to protect the flocks from the winter winds) and many of them were built only in the last few years – though to a traditional design.

Eventually, you will reach the point at Punta Nati, a desolate place where the rocks plunge headlong into the ocean. There is no parking area here and the lane is a narrow dead-end, but a footpath leads down the side of the lighthouse to the cliff edge.

From here you can walk along the cliff-tops east to the three dramatic inlets of Cala es Pous, Cala es Morts and Colodar de Torre Nova, where you can watch gulls swooping across the water. The route eventually leads across rough terrain east to Cala Morell after around 6km; you will not find any refreshments here, so make sure you have at least a supply of drinking water.

The Calas of the Southwest

East of Cala'n Bosc and west of Cala de Santa Galdana lie some of the most beautiful natural calas on the island – tiny rocky inlets, some with a rug-sized patch of sand at their head and others, wider stretches of moon-shaped strands.

A coastal path runs the 10 or so kilometres between the two resorts, making for an excellent day hike

(though sections of the route are steep).
Public transport between the two is not
very convenient, with a stop at Ferreries
and again at Ciutadella.

Some of the best beaches can be
reached down lanes or tracks only if you
have your own transport. The most
famous of these is Cala en Turqueta,
now considered the most beautiful in
Menorca for its diminutive size, fine
white sand and backing of pines. The
road from the Ermita de Sant Joan de
Missa (*see p134*) leads on south to the
beach and you will need to drive
through a farm gate to reach the parking
area (*parking charge*). From here you
can pick up sections of the footpath
along to Cala Macarella to the east
(around 3km) or climb the peak of Talia
d'Artrutx (83m).

Further east are two contrasting
beaches. The tiny pearl of Cala de Talaia
(just west of Talia d'Artrutx) and the
neighbouring Platjes de Son Saura, a
long stretch of west-facing sand backed
by extensive sand dunes that gets
sunlight late into the day. Behind the
Son Saura beach is a large reed bed and
marshland, which offers ideal conditions
for water birds, insects and reptiles,
particularly large dragonflies and
butterflies; nature lovers can spend a few
hours relaxing here. Carrying a pair of
binoculars will prove very useful here.

These beaches are most easily reached
from an intersection off the
Ciutadella/Cala'n Bosc road at So
n'Olivar Vell that leads to Torre Saura;
you may be required to park the car at
the Torre Saura farm (*parking charge*)

A stone sheep pen in Punta Nati

and walk the final 2km to the beach.

The Northwest Coast

Between Cala Morell and the cape at Cavalleria is a stretch of coastline with little vehicular access. The land here is dotted with small farmsteads but there are no towns and villages – just a maze of country lanes and compacted dirt tracks with a few road signs. This is way off the tour group itinerary but makes ideal walking country if you carry a picnic lunch. The western beach of Cala Algaiarens and the eastern Platja de Binimel·là, both excellent beaches, mark the border access points, but the more you enter the hinterland the more you will find that the coastline turns rocky.

Castell de Santa Àgueda, a couple of kilometres inland from the beach, is certainly worth a visit, though the walk to the remains takes about an hour. This is Menorca's second highest peak, and a strategic lookout point over the whole of the north coast. The castle was built by the Moors on Roman foundations. Roman governors spent their summers here because the air was cooler, and it was here the Arabs

Sanitja Dock

THE CAMI DES CAVALLS

Although British Governor Kane built the first cross-country road during his tenure in the early 18th century, travel around the island was still difficult. Most locals used boats and the sea was their highway.

When the French took over the island they created a bridle path all the way around the coastline. This allowed them to set up a warning system in case of attack whereby riders could gallop to the next guard station to warn of danger. Sections of the Cami des Cavalls, or Horse Road as the locals call it, were used until Franco's time, but many remote sections fell into disuse soon after they were created.

There is now a long-term plan to reinstate the Cami for leisure use. You can already enjoy certain such sections at Es Grau (see p88), though it may be some time before you can follow in French footsteps and walk or cycle around the fringes of the island.

retreated to, to make a last stand during Alphonso's campaign in 1287. The fort was used by the Christian conquerors who built a small church that today lies in ruins overgrown by foliage; however, the paved route to the summit is almost totally intact.

Castell de Santa Àgueda. Off the ME-1 road west of Ferreries, signposted Santa Teresa. Open access. Admission free.

The Wild Southwest

The country lanes of the southwestern corner of Menorca lead to historical sites such as Ermita de San Joan de Missa (*see p134*) and Son Catlar (*see p135*). The Artrutx area, as it is known to the locals, is a landscape where you can lose yourself amongst remote farmsteads and ancient remains. There

Off the beaten track

Exploring the caves

is an excellent cross-country walk from the hermitage to the tiny bay at Cala Macarella (where there is a café in summer), then up through Barranc de Santa Anna with its archetypal southern landscape and foliage, and around Puig de Son Tica, the highest point in the area at a monumental 92m, before returning to Sant Joan de Missa. You couldn't feel further away from civilisation even though it is less than 30 minutes from Ciutedalla or Cala n'Bosc.

Be prepared

Whatever time of year you head out, it is wise to carry a supply of water in the car or with you when you walk. Many of Menorca's beaches have summer bars where you can get a drink and snacks in high season, but the more remote beaches don't. A picnic or a supply of snacks is a good idea, especially if you are travelling with children.

Shopping

Menorca has a good mix of souvenirs to cater to every budget. Despite its small size it has several craft industries, so it is possible to buy unusual objects and artefacts that you will find only here.

Natural dye T-shirts

T-shirts

T-shirts have become standard souvenirs worldwide but Menorca has turned its back on the mass-produced imported examples. Two companies – Ecòlogica de Menorca and Bini Clothing – produce T-shirts using good-quality cotton, natural dyes and a good range of muted colours and patterns, which are sold in shops and boutiques across the island.

Ceramics

Spain is famous for its ceramics and Menorca has some excellent examples of fired terracotta bowls, pots and jugs to grace your kitchen. The prices are very reasonable, the only problem being how to carry these items back home safely.

Lladro

Lladro porcelain is one of Spain's most famous brands and a collector's dream with thousands of examples in the catalogue and an ever-changing number of designs in their recognisable pale blue and grey colours.

Although it is not manufactured in Menorca, Lladro can be bought in a number of stores around the island. Castillo Menorca (*Ctr General, the main road across the island, Ciutadella; open:* *daily 10am–10pm*) has one of the finest collections in the whole of Spain, with pieces priced from around 50 euros to over 20,000 euros.

Leather Goods

Menorca has a long history of fine work in leather and the tradition carries on today with a small but thriving shoe industry (*see pp152–3*). Companies like Jaime Mascaró in Ferreries (factory shop) and Poligon Industrial (*on the main road; tel: 971 37 45 00; open: Mon–Fri 9.30am–8pm, Sat 9.30am–1.30pm & 4.30–8pm*) produce high fashion shoes and clothing for the top end of the market.

Menorcan sandals (*see p153*) are an excellent and practical souvenir, and you can buy them in all the major towns.

The mass-produced leather goods you see in the market are not usually made in Menorca; they are more often imported from Africa or the Far East.

Edibles and Imbibeables (or Food and Drink)

Xoriguer gin in its ceramic bottles and other liqueurs have been made on the island since the 18th century. Or, you can take home some of Menorca's famous cheese, dried sausage or ham (all prepacked for travelling).

Where to Shop
Markets

The Menorcan market, as in many other parts of Spain, has a long tradition. It used to bring families into town from the surrounding countryside once a week to sell their produce, buy provisions and catch up with the latest comings and goings on the island. Today it continues to be a colourful affair, though the old knife-grinder may be out of business and much of the wares are being aimed at tourists, certainly in the summer. Markets start early, often around 8am, and by 2pm the stall-holders are packing up their goods.

Market Days

Alaior – *c/Pare Huguet; Thur.*
Ciutadella – *Plaça d'es Born; Fri & Sat.*
Es Castell – *Plaça de s'Esplanada; Mon & Wed.*
Es Migjorn Gran – *Plaça de l'Església; Wed.*
Es Mercadal – *Plaça Pare Camps; Sun.*
Ferreries – *Plaça d'Espanya; Fri.* Craft market – *Sat.*
Fornells – *c/Mar; Thur.*
Maó – *Plaça de s'Esplanada; Tue & Sat.*
Collector's Market – *Claustre del Carme; Sat 6–8pm.*
Punta Prima – *Passeig Maritim; Mon, Wed, Sat & Sun.*
Sant Lluis – *Plaça de la Creu; Mon & Wed.*

Shops

For the best shopping, head to the major towns of Maó and Ciutadella, whose streets have a mixture of high-quality and budget options. The major resorts tend to cater to beachgoing visitors, and offer blow-up sunbeds, snorkels, flippers and 'must-have' other paraphernalia, plus mass-produced

A shop displaying Panama hats and shoes

souvenirs. Try the shops below for good-quality souvenirs.

Don't forget that shops are usually closed for siesta between 1pm and 5pm, and many stay closed on Sundays (in tourist resorts they may be open throughout the day and on Sundays).

Alaior
M Isabel de Salort Pons
Handmade dolls in traditional Menorcan costume are a cottage industry here. A must for doll collectors or anyone looking for a unique gift/souvenir.
Plaça Constitució 1.
Tel: 971 37 11 31.

Ciutadella
Davant
Davant sells all kinds of clothing including linens and T-shirts, plus genuine Panama hats – perfect for the Menorcan climate. It is housed in a historic building next to the cathedral.
Praza Catedral 7.
Tel: 971 38 58 89.

Marina Juanico
This young jeweller creates signature pieces with an accent on impact. They work well with any wardrobe.
Seminari 38.
Tel: 971 48 08 79.

Ciutadella has high-quality shopping including perfume stores

A tourist shops at a local market in Ciutadella

Es Castell
Tekina

A tiny boutique selling a range of ladies' clothing – whatever is in fashion during the season but not too trendy.
Moll de Cales Fonts 20 (on the harbourfront).
Tel: 971 35 35 53.

Ferreries
Nuria Deya Molina

A jewellery designer who works mostly in precious metals to produce modern accent pieces.
Sant Bartomeu 46, 2b.
Tel: 971 37 35 23.

Fornells
Boga Boga

A lovely boutique selling ladies' fashion garments and accessories with just the right look for the summer.

C/Poeta Riera 2.
Tel: 971 37 63 93.

La Mola
Fortesa Isabel II

There is an excellent gift shop featuring branded fort goods from candles and pencils to mugs and T-shirts. These often have colourful stylised images of soldiers dressed in scarlet uniforms.
La Mola.
Tel: 971 41 10 66.

Maó
S'Alambic

There are several large souvenir shops in the port but this is the largest and has an excellent range including ceramics, glass, wooden objects and clothing, and the ubiquitous Menorcan sandals.
Moll de Ponent 36, Port de Maó.
Tel: 971 35 07 07.

Santi Capó

Simple gold and silver jewellery using ultra-modern designs.
Rector Mort 22b.
Tel: 971 36 63 40.

Monte Toro (Es Mercadal)
Monte Toro Souvenirs

A large shop with a good selection of souvenirs.
Monte Toro. Tel: 971 15 40 01.

Ceràmiques Lora produces traditional ceramic objects using old Menorcan techniques. Items include garlic, oil and cheese storage containers, and flasks carried into the fields by farmers before the invention of plastic bottles. The workshop is in the same complex as the S'Alambic shop (*see above*). *Tel: 971 35 03 03.*

Tanning was an important industry throughout the Balearics during the era of the Moors. But the footwear industry really took off in the late 19th century. Within a couple of decades, leather footwear was the mainstay of the Menorcan economy and a third of the population was employed in the industry.

The first factories were founded at Ciutadella. However, they were soon established in the inland towns as well. It was not long before the 'zapata a la mahonesa' or 'shoe of Mahon', then made of dark leather decorated with a silver buckle, was considered the height of fashion across Europe in the ready markets of France and England.

During the 20th century, mass production hit the island hard. Cheaper and inferior-quality products flooded the European markets and many Menorcan factories, with their high labour overheads, went out of business.

However, those that survived are thriving to this day. They have done this by coming full circle and concentrating on the aspect of the industry that won them customers 100 years ago – quality. They have made sure that they are positioned in the upmarket sector of the industry, making shoes and accessories for designer labels such as Pierre Cardin.

Footwear made in Menorca is still exported around the world along with high-quality leather clothing and accessories such as handbags, wallets and briefcases. You can shop in one of the fine boutiques in Maó or Ciutadella, or visit the factory shops for bargains.

Fratelli Rossetti
Shoe manufacturer
Miguel de Cervantes 46, Alaior.
Tel: 971 37 11 44.

Jaime Mascaró

High-class fashionable leather shoes and clothes.
C/Ses Moreres 29, Maó.
Tel: 971 36 05 68 (also at the airport).
Factory shop details in shopping section.

Pons Quintana

Quality leather shoes and accessories.
S'Arraveleta 21, Maó. Tel: 971 35 58 51.

AVARQUES

The other side of the shoe industry is the opposite of this international market. Rustic, yet elegant sandals, the *avarques* are unique to Menorca. They were originally designed for the farm worker, being both comfortable and hard-wearing, but today they are trendy and are worn by everyone.

The simple uppers, with a swatch of natural tanned 'nubuck' leather across the bridge of the foot and a slong of the same leather behind the heel, is sewn to the sole with sturdy twine. The sole combines soft suede under the foot with a layer of car tyre rubber underneath. This was originally meant to give the wearer grip on uneven terrain.

There are several producers of *avarques* on the island and several have got together to protect the quality of the product, forming the Associación de Fabricantes de Calzado de Menorca.

Two artisans who still produce by hand are:

Ca'n Doblas

Using the same traditional raw materials and range of colours.
Plaça Jaume II 1, Ferreries.
Tel: 971 15 50 21.

Uris Mercadal S.L.

Uris puts his own interpretation on the sandal. The style remains the same but the materials, patterns and colours are unique to him – so the normally neutral-coloured *avarques* are produced in pinks, purples and blues.
Plaça Jaume II 10, Ciutadella.
Tel: 971 35 57 86.

Fashionable and comfortable, Menorcan sandals (*avarques*) are available all over the island and are a great buy.

Entertainment

BARS, CLUBS AND DISCOS

Somnolent Menorca certainly doesn't have the same reputation as a party island as its larger siblings Ibiza and Mallorca. If you have come for serious clubbing, you're in the wrong place. However, there are one or two late-night venues that can be hunted out, and many large hotels also run discotheques during the peak of the season. The main resort areas have karaoke bars or large-screen TVs that air your favourite soaps and live sports events.

Clubs generally stay open until dawn and don't get busy until around midnight. Do what the locals do: have a late dinner around 10pm and then head to a bar to watch the nightly *paseo* (communal evening stroll). Spaniards go to clubs to be seen, not to drink till they drop – so dressing smartly is *de rigueur* to get into the best local places.

Maó

With the largest population on the island, Maó has the biggest concentration of clubs and disco bars. Many can be found along the waterside molls – pick the style of music you like and follow the beat!

Bar Akelarre

Probably the coolest place on the island with ultra-modern, minimalist styling and cool jazz music.
Moll de Ponent 41–43. Tel: 971 36 50 70.

A British pub in Cala'n Bosc

Si

A long-standing disco-bar with a mainly local clientele.
c/Verge de Gracia. Tel: 971 36 00 04.

Tse Tse

On the old ramp up to the town just off Moll de Ponent, the Tse Tse is an intimate but lively establishment that forms a standard stop-off on the nightly stroll from bar to bar.
Costa des General 14.

Ciutadella

Asere

The premier spot in the city with rooms cut into the cliffs by the harbour.
c/Pere Capllonc 15.
Tel: 971 38 38 52.

Jazzbah

A very cool place with a jazz and blues vibe.
Plaça Sant Joan 3 (just inland from the port). Tel: 971 48 53 29.

Lateral

More rock and techno, and next door to Jazzbah.
Plaça Sant Joan. Tel: 971 48 40 50.

Cala'n Porter

Cova d'en Xoroi

Without doubt the most famous and coolest club on the island, set in the vast cave complex above the resort of Cala'n Porter. Guest DJs appear throughout the summer and there are foam parties plus different themes throughout the week.
Cala'n Porter. Tel: 971 37 70 64.
www.covadenxoroi.com.
Open: nights mid-May–mid-Sept.

A 24-hour video rental store

Sant Climent

Casino Sant Climent

Excellent jazz club with regular live sessions; if you play an instrument you can join in the jam sessions.
c/Sant Jaume 4. Tel: 971 15 34 18.

Sant Lluis

Lasala

This tapas bar-cum-gastronomic restaurant at the Son Tretze Hotel has developed into a kind of cultural centre famed for its live traditional music and regular exhibitions. The programme changes constantly, so check the website.
Binifadet 20. Tel: 971 15 09 43.
www.amaca.com

CASINOS
Casino Maritim

The only casino on the island also has a bar and restaurant. It is a great place for a little fling at the gaming tables and slot machines, but don't lose your shirt!

You will need some identification to gain admission, so don't forget your passport or driving licence.
Moll de Llevant 287, Maó.
Tel: 971 36 49 62. Open: 3pm–5am.

HORSE SHOWS

The horse has an important place in traditional Catalan and Spanish life, and is an emblem at many fiesta and religious celebrations. This is seen at its best in the Sant Joan procession that takes place on the 23rd June at Ciutadella (*see p133*).

If you are not on the island at the time of this unique event, there are two companies that run shows throughout the year. Both offer a rousing spectacle and are interesting for all ages. The two companies have show rings only a couple of hundred metres apart in the centre of the island, but offer shows on different nights.

Club Escola Menorquina (*Caretta Cala Galdana, Ferreries; tel: 971 15 50 59; www.showmenorca.com*) is a family-owned company that has been running shows for over 25 years. These feature traditional precision horsemanship including demonstrations of how the horses are specially trained for the Menorcan fiestas, and several special tricks including horses who can disco dance (*shows: Wed & Sat 8.30pm; admission charge, free for under 12s*).

Son Martorellet Gran Show Equestre

Sant Joan celebrations

(*Carette Cala Galdana km 1.7; tel: 609 04 94 93; www.sonmartorellet.com*) has a slightly different approach with a show of formal dressage and horse skills used on the mainland. The complex also has a small children's playground (*shows: Tue & Thur 8.30pm; admission charge*).

MUSIC

Menorca has several interesting and well-established music festivals.

The main event is the Maó International Music Festival with performances from July to September. The Young Musicians of Maó are regular participants; international orchestras and choirs such as the English Chamber Orchestra and the American Spiritual Ensemble Choir are also invited to perform. Venues include the Església Santa Maria and Teatro Principal.

The Menorcan Jazz Festival is held in

May with performances at venues across the island, such as in the Cloister of San Francesc Church in Maó, Placa d'Espanya at Ferreries, Placa de Catedral in Ciutadella and in the two island theatres. The festival is sponsored by *Jazz Obert Magazine* (*Jazz Obert; tel: 666 37 39 61; www.jazzobert.com*).

The d'Estiu Music Festival is held in July and August each year in Ciutadella, with the classical chamber and vocal performances usually held in the Claustre del Seminari at 9.30pm. More details can be had from the town Tourist Office or at *www.jjmmciutadella.com* (no information in English).

Ongoing performances

At the Catedral de Menorca in Ciutadella there are organ recitals (*tel: 618 88 75 34; performances: Mon–Sat 11.30am–noon;*

admission charge). Església de Santa Maria in Maó also hosts organ recitals at the same time.

Caneras de S'Hostal quarries at Ciutadella (*Cami Vell; tel: 971 48 15 78*), has a small stone stage that hosts orchestral and musical concerts.

THEATRE AND THE ARTS

The island has two main theatres (*see Culture section for details*) with a full programme of performances throughout the year. Check the box offices for details.

The tourist office prints a weekly list of all cultural activities including concerts, exhibitions and folkloric festivals. Guide tours and special openings for galleries or other attractions are also listed. Pick this up at the airport when you arrive or at a tourist office.

There are spectacular horse shows on the island throughout the year

Children

Menorca is a great place to bring children on holiday. Let us start with the raw materials. The island has guaranteed sunshine from May to September; warm seas for swimming and snorkelling; excellent sandy beaches for building sandcastles or playing beach volleyball; and a range of water sports from pedalos to banana rides. Most of Menorca's beaches (except perhaps Son Bou) are good for little ones because the shallows are gradual with no big waves – perfect for building confidence.

A little boy enjoying his boat ride

Menorca's well-established tourism infrastructure caters well to families. Most large hotel and apartment complexes have swimming pools, with one set aside for children. Kids' clubs and in-complex entertainment ensure

A fun ride at a children's park

that they will rarely be bored and will have somewhere to make new friends. The island's larger western resorts (Cala'n Bosc, Cala'n Blanes and Cala'n Forcat) offer waterparks for those who need 'watery' entertainment.

Getting out on the water on boat trips is great fun for children of all ages and there are glass-bottomed boats that allow them to get a fish's-eye view of life beneath the waves. Older children might like to try diving – the instruction is professional and instructors are English or English-speaking.

Children can spend their well-earned allowances on the latest holiday fashions – like having a temporary henna tattoo or, for the girls, hair braids.

The fiestas that take place across the island throughout the summer will certainly catch their attention with local traditional costumes and dancing. If you can't be there on the 23rd and 24th of June for the famous Sant Joan celebrations in Ciutadella (*see p133*), visit one of the two entertaining horse shows where the animals are put through their paces in preparation for the big day. Kids will be enthralled by the equine tricks – though they may all leave the stadium wanting riding lessons!

The Spanish love children and treat them with indulgence. They are welcomed in restaurants and bars, and are even spirited away by waiters into the kitchens for mama to pat them on the head, and bill and coo over them. Boisterous behaviour is not frowned upon as it is in some other countries, and youngsters are allowed to run around while the adults chat over drinks.

Spanish children regularly stay up until after midnight, especially during the long summer holidays, but don't forget that they will have had at least

two hours' sleep during the traditional afternoon siesta in the heat of the early afternoon. It may be wise to get your little ones into the same habit if you want to have an evening out in Spanish style.

A word about the hot sun

Don't forget to keep young skin well creamed as the sun is very strong here, especially between June and September. Always put cream on children after they have been swimming. Make sure they wear a hat and carry a long-sleeved item of clothing just in case you need to cover sunburned limbs. Children also need to be kept well hydrated in the hot weather. They may not complain about feeling thirsty but regular drinks are the order of the day.

Building sandcastles at the beach

Sport and Leisure

There is plenty to do on the island, though many of the activities are water-based. The nice thing is that some of the most satisfying activities don't cost the earth and you can get to see the best that Menorca has to offer under your own steam. Organised activities are professionally managed, and most guides and instructors speak good English.

A speedboat

SPECTATOR SPORTS

The football-crazy Catalans have no team in Menorca, though Mallorca has a successful one. Instead, the island follows the action on TV. Some of the spectator sports on offer are as below.

Hippodrome

Between Maó and Sant Lluis you will find a hippodrome where there are trotting races (with horses pulling two-wheeled lightweight carriages) every weekend in the early evenings (*Carreras*

Taking a trip on the blue Mediterranean

de Caballos Al Trote; tel: 971 36 57 31; racing currently starts at 5.30pm). There is also a track at Ciutadella.

Golf

The course at Son Parc is not on the grand international tour but hosts the Menorca Men's Open Championship during the middle of May for a week. Later in the year it runs more competitions during 'October Golf Week' (usually at the beginning of the month). There are local competitions each weekend and if you have a handicap you don't have to watch, you can enter!
Amistosa Campo de Golf, Urbanización Son Parc. Tel: 971 18 88 75. www.clubsonparc.com

Sailing Regattas

There are several throughout the year in the waters around the island. Watching the action is difficult from the land, but when the boats dock at the end of the racing day the atmosphere along the harbour front is magical.

The most important is the Menorca Sant Joan Regatta to coincide with the Sant Joan celebrations on 23rd and 24th

Kayaking is another way of getting to the island's remote areas

June. Boats sail from Barcelona to the port of Maó. The King's Cup for 'period' boats held in late August is a colourful meet with antique and classic vessels.

Running
The Ciutadella half-marathon, usually held on 1st October, is accompanied by a fiesta.

SPORTS AND ACTIVITIES
Boat trips
Heading out onto the warm waters of the Mediterranean is one of the pleasures of a trip to Menorca, and many of the island's remote coves can only be reached by boat. There are numerous organised day trips from tourist harbours with swimming included. Simply take along your swimsuits, get a feel of what it is really like on the high seas and enjoy.

Blue Mediterranean
Take an afternoon's sail on a 75ft catamaran (*trips depart: from the harbour at Maó; Tue–Sun 10.15am; lunch included*). For a more private experience, the company offers a full or half-day charter or champagne lunch with a range of boats to suit all budgets, tastes and group sizes.
Offices at Port de Maó, port de Ciutadella, port at Fornells, marina at Cala'n Bosc, and the marina at Cala de Santa Galdana.
Tel: 609 30 53 14.
www.chartermenorca.com

Fornells
Catamaran Charter
A great trip along the north shore of the island.
Maritimo des Fornells.
Tel: 628 48 64 26.
www.catamarancharter.net

Cycling
Quiet and relatively flat roads away from the main roads offer some lovely cycling routes. From Ciutadella north to the cluster of resorts around Cala'n Forcat or south to Cala'n Bosc, even beginners won't get out of breath. There are similar runs around Fornells and Arenal d'en Castell or to Es Grau. It is a little more challenging inland and amongst the barrancs of the south coast resorts, where the way down is easy but you have no option but to pedal up on the way out.

If you are an experienced mountain biker, the narrow country lanes and walking trails offer the most adventure, but it is the beautiful remote surroundings rather than the degree of difficulty that is the draw here.

Adventure Sports offers guided mountain bike treks; or you can hire a bike and set off on your own adventure.
Passeig Maritim 44b, Fornells (on the waterfront). Tel: 609 67 09 96.
www.diacomplert.net

In late October the Menorcan Touring Cycling Association (*www.ciclomenorca.com*) organises the 'Vuelta Cicloturistica' – a three-stage race that is open to everyone.

You can even hire a pedal-boat with a waterslide!

Fishing in shallow waters

Diving

Menorca has worked hard to maintain the quality of its marine environment and certainly has something to offer every diver from caves to shipwrecks. The quality of the diving training is good, and qualified divers can choose from several locations for guided or accompanied dives.

Most diving companies run an 'introduction to diving' day package that is a kind of appetiser session. To gain the 'Open Water Certificate', the first stage qualification, usually takes around five days of study and practical training.

Fornells
Diving Centre Fornells

Offers training and diving equipment on rental plus a range of underwater day excursions.
PADI Open water course 435, Discover Scuba 65.

Passeig Maritim. Tel: 971 37 64 31.
www.divingfornells.com

S'Algar
S'Algar Diving Menorca

Professional and long-running company that offers a range of water-based activities including diving training, parascending, snorkelling instruction and guided tours, and powerboat lessons. You can also rent equipment if you are already qualified. The main dives take place at 10am and 2.30pm with departures throughout the day on the hour during July and August.
S'Algar. Tel: 971 15 06 01.
www.salgardiving.com

Addaia
ULMO Diving Addaia

Good diving outfit on the north coast with diving instruction and guided dives.
Port of Addaia. Tel: 971 35 90 05.
www.ulmodiving.com

Glass-Bottomed Boat Trips

If swimming under the waves isn't for you, it is still possible to enjoy the varied sea life around the Menorcan coast on a glass-bottomed boat trip. The viewing windows allow you to catch sight of shoals of fish and crustaceans on the rocky bottoms with a very occasional dolphin on view.

Amigos

Runs trips with stops for swimming; the boat has a waterslide and a bar/café.
Cala'n Bosc. Tel: 618 34 80 06.
Trips: daily in season 9am & 2pm.
Tickets must be purchased at least an hour before departure.

Don Joan

A sightseeing tour of the outer harbour at Maó including a commentary on land-based buildings like the Lazaretto quarantine hospital and the English Cemetery. This is the largest craft offering this round-the-harbour trip. On other days the boat heads for swimming trips up the coast around Es Grau to the north or Binibèquer in the south.
Port de Maó. Tel: 971 35 07 78.
Harbour tours: Tue & Sat 11.30am, 1pm & 2.30pm. Coastal tours: Apr–Oct Mon, Wed–Fri & Sun 9.45am & 2.45pm.

Yellow Catamarans

The same tour as Don Joan but in a cute yellow craft.
Port de Maó. Tel: 639 67 63 51.
Departures: every 45mins from 10.30am–3.30pm, May–Oct Sun 10.45am, 12.15pm & 1.45pm.

Golf

Surprisingly, there is only one golf course on the island and it is located at Son Parc on the north coast. The golf school has English-speaking teachers and 'Swingcam' stance analysis to improve your game. Children's lessons are also provided.
Amistosa Campo de Golf, Urbanización Son Parc. Tel: 971 18 88 75.
www.clubsonparc.com

Horse riding

The country lanes that crisscross Menorca make excellent bridle paths and seeing the country from the back of a horse gives you a great perspective.

Snorkelling is an excellent way to spot local marine life

Boating is a great way to view the coastline

Menorca a cavall (*24km Ciutadella/Maó Road, just west of Es Mercadal; tel: 626 59 37 37*) has horses for hire and also guided trekking.

Sea Kayaking

With benign summer waters and miles of breathtaking coastline to explore, it is not surprising that sea kayaking has become popular very quickly here. If you need some training, the bay at Fornells is the perfect location; once you have got your sea legs you are free to explore the caverns and remote bays that you can't reach by road.

Adventure Sports (*see Cycling*) offers accompanied sea kayaking safaris around the Menorca coastline or kayaks on hire if you are already proficient.

Snorkelling

This easy-to-do sport can be undertaken without supervision; just make sure that kids know how to breathe through the tube. You can swim out along the banks of the calas to spot shrimp, crabs, the occasional squid or octopus, and, of course, lots of fish. It is a wonderfully relaxing way to spend a couple of hours.

Walking and hiking

Menorca has no high mountains and a network of well-marked walking routes, so it is an excellent environment for beginners. There is lots of variation including coastal and inland routes with ancient remains and rural lifestyles to explore. There are also lots of hidden coastal beaches that can only be reached on foot or by boat. The solitude and magnificent scenery are a real incentive to head out on the trail.

If you would prefer walking with a guide, Adventure Sports (*see cycling*) offers trekking and hiking with routes to suit the fitness levels of the clients.

Windsurfing

One of the best places in the Mediterranean to learn to windsurf is in the bay of Fornells. The wide shallow waters and prevailing breezes offer ideal conditions and the instruction is excellent. If you already know how to windsurf, there are plenty of rental boards here for you to get out on the water and enjoy.

When to go
Most high-energy or extreme sports are best undertaken in the spring and autumn when temperatures drop from the stifling July to August peaks. Even so, whatever time of year you intend being active, take plenty of water, a high factor sun cream and suitable clothing including sensible footwear and a hat.

For something a little different, try swapping your land-based holiday in a hotel, apartment or villa for a water-based stay. The magnificent coastline and easy passage to the sister Balearic islands of Ibiza, Mallorca and Formentera, combined with benign summer waters, make Menorca a prime sailing destination of the world.

You don't even need to head out of Menorcan waters to get the benefit of a sailing holiday. Some of the island's most unspoilt calas can be reached only by boat or on foot, and there can be no better feeling than dropping anchor at your own private cove surrounded by crystal-clear azure waters with a hint of golden sand, where the only sound you will hear is the lapping of the waves.

MARINAS

Marinas in Menorca vary in size and in facilities. The most basic ones offer berths and fresh water, while the most modern will have electrical connections for boats, shower facilities and even accommodation. The ports are well organised for the yachting crowd. The most romantic are those where you can disembark and sit on the quayside enjoying an aperitif or dinner at a restaurant overlooking the yachts.

Popular ports of call
Addaia
Ciutadella
Maó
Cala'n Bosc
Cala de Santa Galdana

GETTING ORGANISED

A popular choice for beginners or those wanting a social trip is the flotilla holiday. This involves groups of boats sailing together on a set route, usually with a guide. If you have a day skipper's certificate (*see below*) you will be allowed to take a boat yourself (a bare boat). With no certificate you will need to hire a captain.

Sunsail have a good deal of experience in holiday provision for both flotilla and bare-boat yachting. Contact them at:

only) in local waters (not too far from the shore, not out in the open ocean) and requiring only basic navigational skills, in moderate wind and sea conditions. Normally, study for the certificate takes 5 days or 3 weekends, with a written test at the end.

The Port House, Port Solent, Portsmouth, Hampshire. PO6 4TH. Tel: 0870 777 0313. Fax: 023 9221 9827. www.sunsail.com

Menorca has a multitude of companies offering boat rentals, package tours or crewed boats for those with or without a day skipper's certificate. Blue Mediterranean offers crewed and bare boats (yachts and catamarans) from around 9m to 23m. *Port de Maó. Tel: 971 36 44 82. www.chartermenorca.com*

TRAINING
The Day Skipper Certificate

This card allows 'the skipper' to be responsible for the safety of his/her boat and crew for day sailing (in daylight

There are a variety of yachts and boats provided by tour companies

Menorca Cruising School and Yacht Charter

This company offers sailing training from a 'Try a big boat for a day' introduction to sailing for complete novices, a 2-day 'Start Yachting' course to 5-day Royal Yachting Association approved courses. Instructors are all English or speak excellent English. Once qualified, they have boats for hire.
Tel: 971 35 41 03.
www.menorcasailing.co.uk

SOMETHING WITH MORE OOMPH!

If sailing isn't for you, perhaps a trip along the coastline in a powerboat is more your style. P&F rent 4–6-man examples for a family day out.
Aquiler de Barcos, harbour, Cala'n Bosc. Tel: 610 26 12 91.
www.barcosdealquiler.com

Birdwatching

The Parc Naturel de s'Albufera Es Grau is the only protected region on Menorca but the rest of the island is also an important birding site for both native species and visiting breeders from the north and south, plus migrants crossing the Mediterranean in the spring and autumn.

Let us start with the Parc Naturel. This is a multi-environment region including woodland, meadows and a 70-hectare freshwater lagoon, which acts as a magnet for fowl like coots, mallards and pochards, and wading birds such as herons and egrets. These include the numerous

cattle egret and blue heron, but also the rarer night and squacco herons. Stilts are also common in the muddy shallows.

The woodlands are home to many species including the tiny firecrest, the smallest European bird. Warblers and crakes can usually be heard rather than seen, and this is especially true of the polyphonic nightingale. Various species of owl hunt by night, while during the day you may see the elegant flight of the booted eagle as it swoops low across the water.

During spring and autumn, the park is teeming with life. It acts as a welcome stop-over for many species on longer journeys north or south.

Another enclosed cove, this time with high cliffs, is the inlet at Cala de Santa Galdana. Warblers including Cettis and nightingales are abundant here, and it is also a nesting site for thousands of swifts who stay for the summer.

The reed beds at Son Bou are the largest such environment, though there are several smaller beds dotting the island. Warblers are the most common species here, including the common great reed warbler. The multicoloured bee-eater is one of Menorca's spectacular migratory birds, arriving every year from the Sahara.

The Cap de Cavalleria region is less settled by man than other parts of the island, and there are several good vantage points to watch curlews and ospreys, plus the Audouin's Gull, one of the world's rarest gull species.

Head to the Punta de S'Escullar in the far northwest to find the nesting areas of the Balearic shearwater and the heavier Corys, both large seabird species that spend much of their lives out at sea. The cliffs are also home to Alpine swifts and a few Egyptian vultures, called miloca by locals.

Menorca has a particularly varied population of predator birds for such a small island. Although pressure on their habitat has reduced the numbers, you can sure to see at least one large raptor. We have already mentioned the Egyptian vulture, the booted eagle and the osprey and the red kite which also catch the thermals, while smaller falcons, kestrels and marsh harriers hunt in the lower skies and across the fields.

USEFUL ORGANISATIONS
Adventure Sports
Offers specialist birdwatching tours.
Passeig Maritim 44b, Fornells.
Tel: 609 67 09 96. www.diacomplert.net

The website *www.birdingpal.org* puts avid birders around the world in touch with one another to share information and meet up for organised activities.

The Royal Society for the Protection of Birds (RSPB)
Information and activities for birdwatchers with affiliations to international organisations.
The Lodge, Sandy, Beds, SG19 2DL.
Tel: 01767 680551.
www.rspb.org.uk

Menorca is an important site for birdwatching

Food and Drink

Being a small island surrounded by water, it is no surprise that the seafood in Menorca is always fresh and varied: grilled (la plancha) sardines, swordfish and other whole fish, or shrimps flambéd for something a little more exotic. Squid or shellfish are also popular. *Caldereta de Llangosta* (a rich stew with lobster meat) is the *pièce de résistance* of Menorcan fish cuisine, and Fornells has a particular reputation for the dish which is priced at around 60 euros per person. The cheaper *caldetera de pescado* (stew of mixed fish) is also delicious.

Es Cranc restaurant, Fornells

For meat eaters too, the island offers a good variety. Succulent beef and lamb are supplemented by game such as rabbit, partridge and quail. Barbecuing is the most popular method of cooking, but there are also a good number of slow-cooked stews that have traditionally seen the population through the cooler winter months.

Island specialities include *sopas mallorquinas* (a thick soup with garlic, olives, vegetables and occasionally pork) and the ubiquitous *quesa de Mahon*,

Fish stew is popular in the slightly cooler months

Menorcan cheese (*see pp118–19*), plus a range of air-dried hams and salamis. *Paella* is also on many menus. This traditional dish of rice, beans and peppers flavoured with saffron featuring both meat and seafood is the most famous dish of mainland Spain. *Tapas* – small 'bites' of various tasty dishes – aren't as popular as on mainland Spain, but they are available and make a good snack or can be ordered in multiples to make up a main meal. Try potatoes with garlicky *aioli* – the precursor to mayonnaise or *mahonesa* as it was originally known.

Vegetarian Food

Non-meat eaters won't have a problem, as the fresh seafood is delicious and served all around the island. Many *tapas* are non-meat items and you can easily find non-meat pastas and pizzas, but be aware that even if a restaurant is willing to serve you *paella* without the chicken, the dish will probably have been cooked in chicken stock. The same may be true of some soups, though the locals have a range of very good non-meat versions.

Vegans may have more of a problem. *Tumbet* – a stew of vegetables in tomato sauce or *Samfiana* (*see below*) are possibilities but that's probably about it. Good salads are getting easier to come by but are normally served as an accompaniment to a main dish; however, most restaurants are happy to accommodate your requests.

Drinks
Spanish coffee (*café*) is short, strong and black, ask for a 'café grande con leche' if you want a longer milkier version.

Beer (*cervesa*) is a pilsner type – look for the Spanish San Miguel, which is always served ice-cold.

For something a little stronger, Xoriguer produce a range of gins and liqueurs (*see p148*). Spanish wine is excellent and not overpriced including the bubbly cava. Spanish brandy, coñac, tends to be a little softer and fruitier than the French variety; you can also enjoy a Spanish sherry – a fortified wine that can run from bone dry to very sweet.

Enjoying the food and weather at an outdoor café

When to Eat
The Spanish traditionally eat dinner around 1pm, then head inside for a siesta. They don't eat dinner until late, normally around 10pm and most restaurants outside the tourist resort areas won't open until 8pm. If you want authentic Spanish atmosphere try to hold your hunger pangs until the late evening.

COMMON FOOD TERMS	
Carne	meat
Peix	fish
Huevos	eggs
Queso	cheese
Arros	rice
Fruta	fruit
Verduras	vegetables
Jamon	ham
Chorizo	spicy sausage
Bocadillos	sandwiches
Estramesos	plate of meats and cheeses
Carn d'oila	soup of different meats
Escudella	vegetable soup
Samfiana	slow cooked onions, peppers, aubergines and tomatoes
Sopas mallorquinas	vegetable soup (sometimes has meat)
Arros negra	rice cooked with black squid ink
Arros a banda	rice with seafood
Paella	aromatic rice and vegetables cooked with seafood such as shrimp and mussels (sometimes chicken)
Sobrasada	spicy pork sausage
Greixonera de peix	fish stew
Panades sobrasada	savoury pastry with meat or fish
Xurros	sweet fried doughnuts served on sticks

Grilled sardines and chips

There's certainly no shortage of pseudo British and Euro-cuisine in the major resorts. The curry, schnitzel and pizza menu they provide is pretty much of a standard. However, here are some eateries that are well worth seeking out if you are touring around the island. The following price guide is for dinner for one person without drinks:

★   under €20
★★   €20–€30
★★★   €30–€40
★★★★   €over 40

Alaior

Cobblers Brasserie ★★★/★★★★
Set in a former cobbler's house (hence the name), this English-owned brasserie has built a tremendous reputation with locals and ex-pats for its excellent cuisine, including some good vegetarian options plus its fine wines. There is a large patio and shady courtyard for outside dining.
San Macario 6. Tel: 971 37 14 00. www.cobblers.es. Open: May–Oct Mon–Sat 7pm–late.

Maó

La Minerva ★★★★
One of the smartest restaurants in town with a harbourfront terrace, so you can watch the 'yachties' at play. The menu of the day (*menu de dià*) is excellent value and the perfect place to lunch after a morning's sightseeing. Reservations recommended.
Moll de Llevant 87. Tel: 971 35 19 95. Open: daily 12.30–3.30pm & 8–11.30pm.

Ciutadella

Aurora ★★
Set on a small lively square five minutes from the cathedral past the Ses Voltes shops, Aurora serves a good selection of well-priced *tapas* plus a range of grilled meat and seafood.
Plaça de Ses Palmeres (Plaça d'Alfons III), Ciutadella. Tel: 971 38 00 29. Open: 9am–after midnight. Restaurant open: daily noon–3pm & 7pm–closing time.

Bar Hogar del Pollo ★
Not the usual kind of tourist restaurant, this no frills bar is where the locals come for some genuine tapas, a glass of country wine and a bit of a gossip; for local atmosphere come here.
Plaza San Pedro 11. Tel: 971 38 33 70. Open: Mon–Sat noon–2pm & 7–11pm.

Es Castell

Sa Torre des Sol ★★★/★★★★
Set in an 18th-century house, Sa Torre des Sol brings some very modern touches to Menorcan cuisine and is frequented by a young urbane crowd. The food is served in several intimate

though minimalist dining rooms. Fixed menu at lunchtimes.
Carrer Victori 54. Tel: 971 36 03 99. www.satorredessol.com. Open: daily 1–3pm & 8–11pm.

Es Grau
Café d'en Moro ★
Simple café with small terrace overlooking the port at Es Grau with excellent tapas and bocadillas. A very relaxed lunch stop.
On the harbourfront. No phone. Open: daily 8am–9pm.

Ferreries
Mesón El Gallo ★★★
Set in a traditionally styled whitewashed 200 year old Menorcan farmhouse, this restaurant has been run by the same family for over 30 years. Its home-style cooking using the best local meats and signature dishes include steak with cheese sauce.
Carretera Cala Galdana km 1.5. Tel: 971 37 30 39. Open: Tue–Sun 1.30–3pm & 7.30–11pm.

Fornells
Es Cranc ★★/★★★★
Most people who visit Fornells are attracted to the seafront restaurants, but this beautifully styled traditional dining room just a couple of minutes along the route to the Fornells tower offers excellent seafood including live crab and lobster plus delicious *Caldereta de Llangosta*. Good service.
Calle Escoles 31. Tel: 971 37 64 42. Open: 1–3.30pm & 8–11pm. Closed: Mon during off-season.

Sant Lluis
Restaurante Pan y Vino ★★★
An ex-professional musician turned wine aficionado and his partner offer this very intimate dining experience in a converted Menorcan farmhouse or outside on the garden terrace. The menu is fixed and changed regularly according to what's market fresh. Reservations appreciated.
Camí de la Coixa, Torret de bai. Tel: 610 31 92 79. Open: Apr–Oct Sat–Wed 8–10pm.

Sa Pedrera d'Es Pujol ★★★★
This married couple have created an excellent gastronomic restaurant with pretty indoor dining and open fire for winter and airy outdoor terrace for summer. The menu changes with the seasons and takes only the freshest ingredients, however the signature 'beef Wellington' is always available.
Camí d'es Pujol, Caserío de Torret 23. Tel: 971 15 07 17. www.sapedreradespujol.com Open: Sept–Jun daily 7–11pm; Jul–Aug daily noon–3pm.

Tapas are great snacks

Menorcan Gin

When the British arrived on Menorca they made many far-reaching changes. One simple thing was the development of gin distillation, a product that is still inexorably linked to the island.

Mahon became one of the Royal Navy's primary Mediterranean bases and the port was teeming with personnel. The English sailors that frequented the taverns of Maó during the 18th century were hard drinkers. Back in England the latest fashion was for gin – alcohol produced by distilling malt or grain and infusing juniper berries – but there wasn't a supply in the Balearics and it seems that nothing else would do. Spotting an opportunity to make a killing, the Menorcans began importing the raw materials for gin distillation and set to work satisfying the demand.

There was one huge difference between the gins produced in northern Europe and Mahon gin (as it became known). This local gin used grape distillates mixed with juniper berries and this imparts a different kind of flavour from the very crisp English style. It is more akin to a Dutch 'genever'.

The Xoriguer Brand

The Pons family had been millers on the island and owned a mill called Xoriguer. When they decided to go into the distilling business they named the business after the mill and Distilerias Xoriguer was born.

Miquel Pons Justo (1906–1981) was a

master marketing man before the term was even invented and moved the brand to its dominant position today. He made the decision to continue with the traditional distillation methods and old style pottery jugs called canecas (traditionally these were adopted because they were strong enough to make the sea crossing when the gin was exported).

Xoirguer is still a family-owned business and only the heirs to the legacy know the precise recipe for Xoriguer gin.

Quality Control

The Mahon Gin, made by Xoriguer is one of only two gins in Europe, the other being Plymouth, to have a specific appellation – or EU designation of origin – meaning it can only be made on the island, according to a specific distillation process. This guarantees the quality of the product and protects the product from fraudsters and imitators.

Enjoy!

Xoriguer's complex aromatic flavour and its fruity wine base means that it provides an excellent base for cocktails. Traditionally it is drunk at Menorcan fiestas with homemade lemonade in a drink called pomada or with just a splash of soda water and a slice of lemon in pallofa. It can even be drunk neat over ice.

Xoriguer produce a ready-made pomada so you don't have to mix it yourself. They also produce a range of liqueurs that are unique to the company including Calent and Pago.

Calent is a traditional drink originally made by the farmer's wife in the farmhouse kitchen. It had no set recipe, being an infusion of various wild herbs, aniseed and cinnamon with wine so each batch would taste slightly different. Xoriguer now produce it to a secret but standard recipe.

Pago is a drink brought to the island by the Phoenicians. The heady liqueur has a base of gentian and herbs and is usually mixed four parts gin to one part pago for a refreshing cocktail.

Distilerias Xoriguer: Andén de Poniente 91, 07701 Maó. Tel: 971 36 21 97. www.xoriguer.es

Facing page: Bottles of Mahon gin
This page: Xoriguer

Hotels and Accommodation

Menorca has a good range of accommodation in all price ranges. The problem is that much of it is contracted to the package tourist companies and finding accommodation as an independent traveller can be difficult, especially in summer. High rack rates for walk-in clients can also make it more expensive than say booking a package with flights and accommodation combined.

A sign for agrotourism in the countryside

Most hotels have good facilities. Many are aimed at families, offering kids' clubs and on-site entertainment but you can also find quieter options if you are looking for a more sedate break. Maó and Ciutadella have some urban hotels that are often aimed at business rather than tourist travellers but these could be useful for a base for a couple of days of sightseeing.

A new accommodation phenomenon on the island is agrotourism – where farmhouses or country properties offer B&B accommodation out in the countryside. These can make an excellent alternative to hotel accommodation and have plenty of charm and character. For even more independence Menorca has a good amount of self-catering accommodation with apartments in purpose built complexes or villas with private pools and gardens.

Whatever your choice, Menorca is so small that nowhere is very far for touring purposes. This is one destination where you can have a base in one resort and still be able to easily visit all other parts of the island.

The following list is a mix of urban hotels, tourist complexes and agrotourist accommodation across the island. It is imperative that you make a booking during the peak period (*late Jul–end-Aug*).

Price scales are for a double room and breakfast only unless stated. They do not include flights except for the Thomas Cook properties. Prices are peak season (*Jul–Aug*).

★	up to €100 per night
★★	€100–€150 per night
★★★	over €150 per night

Cala de Santa Galdana
RTM Audax ★★★
Modern high-rise 4-star hotel overlooking the coastal inlet at the far end of Cala de Santa Galdana, the Audax has an excellent 7000sq m state-of-the-art wellness centre and spa to offer you a wonderful place to relax. Rooms are plushly furnished and each has a balcony.
Urb Septenora, Cala de Santa Galdana, 07750 Ferreries. Tel: 971 15 46 46. www.rtmhotels.com

Cala Morell

Biniatram ★

This renovated farmhouse set in 4,000sq m of land has four rooms and two apartments for rent individually, or you can rent the whole farmhouse for a large family or group. Facilities include large pool, tennis court and gardens. Within walking distance of Cala Morell. Breakfast not included in room price.
Biniatram, 07760 Ciutadella.
Tel: 971 38 31 13. www.biniatram.com

Cala'n Bosc

Hotel Miranda Gardens ★★

Brightly painted low-rise apartment complex set amongst verdant gardens, 700m from the beach. The property has lots of facilities for families including a kids' club, pools and a bar lounge and buffet restaurant.
A Thomas Cook property.
Tel: 0870 750 5711.
www.thomascook.co.uk

Ciutadella

Hotel Rural Sant Ignasi ★★★

Set in almost 4 hectares of park and woodland northeast of the town, the Sant Ignasi is a converted 18th century mansion. The 20 rooms are large and individually furnished with period and modern pieces. The communal areas have been well designed to offer a luxurious feel that is carried on through the gastronomic restaurant and onto the terrace and good-sized pool. A beautiful place to relax.
Carretera Cala Morell, Ciutadella.
Tel: 971 38 55 75. www.santignasi.com

The RTM Audax is at the far end of Cala Santa Galdana

Es Castell

Hotel del Almirante ★

A listed 18th-century mansion that once belonged to Admiral Collingwood, the Almirante Collingwood is rather like a country house hotel than a resort hotel, though it does have a pool. Period furnishings add to the atmosphere.
Collingwood House, Carretera Mahon – Es Castell s/n, 07720 Es Castell. Tel: 971 36 27 00. www.hoteldelalmirante.com

Maó

Casa Alberti ★★

Recently refurbished 18th-century town mansion with six minimalist modern rooms plus a communal kitchen and terrace. A good option for a weekend in Maó, on the doorstep of the restaurants and bars.
Isabel II 9, 07701 Maó. Tel: 971 35 41 10. www.casaalberti.com

RTM Capri Hotel ★★★

Modern five-storeyed hotel that makes a good base for touring the city. The seventy five rooms are comfortably furnished in muted but modern style, there is a café bar on site and the hotel has a small spa with pool, jacuzzi and sun terrace on the roof with views across the city.
*San Estaban 8, 07703 Maó.
Tel: 971 36 14 00. www.rtmhotels.com*

Punta Prima

Punta Prima Suites ★★★

Luxuriously furnished suites set in lush private gardens, 150m from the beach; this is the place to come for some

The RTM Capri Hotel

Hotel del Almirante in Es Castell

serious upmarket relaxation. Guests have a restaurant/bar and freeform pool on hand but can use all the facilities of the neighbouring Insotel for a more active break.
C Migjera s/n, Punta Prima, 07713 Ferreries. Tel: 971 15 92 00. www.insotel.com

Sant Tomàs
Hotel Sant Tomàs ★★
This older style property has been thoroughly renovated. It sits in lawned gardens overlooking the sea and there's a wellness and beauty clinic on the premises. Indoor and outdoor pools make it great for early or late season holidays. The facilities and position suits couples over families. Buffet restaurant and bar.
A Thomas Cook property.
Tel: 0870 750 5711.
www.thomascook.co.uk

Sant Lluis
Biniarroca Hotel Rural ★★★
This 15th-century farmhouse has been beautifully decorated and is now Menorca's principal 'boutique' hotel with 18 individually furnished rooms. There is a permanent exhibition of art by Lindsay Mullen here. The property has an outdoor pool, verdant garden and there is a gastronomic restaurant open in the evenings.
Cami Vell 57. Tel: 971 15 00 59.
www.biniarroca.com

Binissafullet Vell ★★
Rural *lloc* (traditional farm) now transformed into a stylish agrotourism B&B with eight individually furnished rooms, a good-sized pool, lounge with library, bar and car park. A lovely place to relax and well placed for touring.
Ctra. Binissafullet 64, Sant Lluis.
Tel: 971 15 66 33. www.binissafullet.com

Son Bou
Sol Pingüinos ★★
It may be a high-rise eyesore but you can't fault this hotel's position right on Menorca's longest stretch of sand with the rest of the quiet resort of Son Bou on the doorstep. The 517 three-star rooms are plainly furnished with balconies, most with a sea view. Good facilities for the whole family.
Playa de Son Bou, Alaior.
Tel: 971 37 12 00. www.solmelia.com

Villa Rental
Menorca Travel (*7a London Road, Alderley Edge, Cheshire SK9 7JT; tel: +44 (0)1625 586337; www.menorcatravel.co.uk*) is a well established company with a good range of villas for rent from two to five or six bedrooms.

Practical Guide

Arriving
Entry Formalities
EU citizens need only a picture ID to gain entry. Residents of the following countries need a valid passport: UK, Australia, Canada, New Zealand and the USA. All other nationalities should consult the nearest Spanish Embassy.

Arriving by Air
Menorca's International Airport (*tel: 971 15 70 00*) is 15 minutes inland from Maó.

Scheduled services: Air Iberia (*www.iberia.es*) is the Spanish national air carrier and it has regular services from Menorca to locations on the other

A road-distance marker

Balearic Islands, on mainland Spain and within Europe. Flights to European cities normally include a transfer in Barcelona. Tickets are flexible and can be for any length of time. British Airways (*www.ba.com*) has some direct flights from London to Menorca, but again, most include a transfer at Barcelona.

If travelling from North America or Australasia, the simplest option would be flights into Spain then a transfer flight on to Menorca. Consult a travel agent or website such as *www.lastminute.com, www.ebookers.com* or *www.expedia.com* for details of routes and fares.

Charter services: There are over 30 direct charter flights a week from airports around the UK to Menorca throughout the summer with services running from April to October for terms of one or two weeks. Contact the major package tourist companies such as Thomas Cook (*tel in the UK: 0870 750 5711; www.thomascook.co.uk*) for more details. These companies sell holiday packages (flight and accommodation) but also sell flight only tickets if you want to arrange your own accommodation.

Arriving by Sea
Transmediterranea (*www.transmediterranea.es*) and Balearia (*www.balearia.net*) both operate vehicle and passenger ferry services from the Spanish mainland to Maó. There are ferry services from Maó and Ciutadella to Alcúdia on Mallorca. Details and times of ferry services may be found in

An inter-island ferry

the *Thomas Cook European Rail Timetable* which is available to buy online from *www.thomascookpublishing.com*, from branches of Thomas Cook in the UK or by telephoning *01733 416477*.

Camping

There are large camp sites at Tori Soli Nou near Son Bou (*tel: 971 37 26 05; open: May–Oct*) and in the hills above Cala de Santa Galdana (*Camping Alalaia; tel: 971 37 30 95; open: May–Oct*).

Climate

Menorca has a Mediterranean maritime climate with hot dry summers and mild winters. The bulk of rainfall takes place between October and December and tends to fall in passing storms.

Weather Conversion Chart
25.4mm = 1 inch
°F = 1.8 x °C + 32

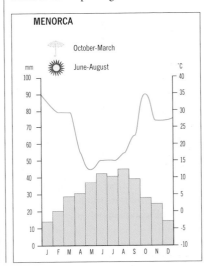

MENORCA

October–March

June–August

Crime

When you visit Menorca you will be at a relatively low risk of being a victim of serious crime, however, so-called petty crime such as theft can be a problem, especially from vehicles. It still pays to take precautions to minimise your chances of a loss.

Do not leave valuables in a car and leave nothing at all on show.

Don't carry large amounts of cash or valuables with you.

Deposit valuables in the hotel safe.

Take extra care at cash point machines: don't allow bystanders to see your PIN (personal identification number).

Put all money away before you leave banks or bureau de change kiosks.

Don't leave valuables unattended in cafés and restaurants.

Customs regulations

The following duty free rules apply for visitors arriving from outside the EU:
200 cigarettes or 250g tobacco
1 litre of spirits or 2 litres of fortified wine
2 litres table wine
There are no currency restrictions.

Usual customs regulations apply for travellers arriving from other EU countries.

Driving

General rules: Drive on the right and pass on the left. Most main roads have good surfaces. Minor roads may be uneven and narrow with limited vision, blind bends and hidden entrances. Road signs and markings comply with the European standard. Alcohol limits are 0.5mg per 100ml of blood. Children should be seated in the back in child seats. Seat belts must be worn by all passengers. Main roads are indicated with ME and a number, though some old signs featuring C and a number are still in use.

Note: When the Spanish flash oncoming traffic it is not a signal for you to proceed. It is a signal that they are coming through.

Speed limits

Urban/villages – 50kph
All other roads – 90kph
Two-lane highways – 120kph
Specific limits may apply especially in towns – always keep an eye on speed signs.

Parking

This is difficult in most large towns. Car parks and most street parking are pay zones – look for blue marking on the surface. Payment is normally 9.30am–1.30pm and 5–9pm (be aware that this is different to the UK with parking tickets required well into the evening) but local regulations may vary so check the machine. Keep small change for meters.

Fuel

Self service fuel (gasolina) stations can be found at all major towns and on the main cross island highway. Note that outside Maó, most close for lunch and siesta between around 1pm to around 4pm so don't plan any afternoon jaunts without checking your fuel level. Petrol stations normally stay open until around 9pm.

Car Rental

A full national or an international driving licence will be needed for rental. Minimum age for rental is 21 with a full licence for at least one year (25 for some companies or types of vehicle). Carry driver's licence and rental document at all times.

Bringing your own vehicle

Carry the registration document, valid insurance and valid licence. It is compulsory to carry two warning triangles in case of accident – these need to be placed some distance in front of and behind the car to warn other traffic.

Electricity

220 volt with European-style two-pin plugs. If you are travelling from the UK you will need an adapter plug.

Embassies

All embassies are located in Madrid on the Spanish mainland:
UK Embassy *c/Fernando el Santo 16. 28010 Madrid. Tel: 91 700 82 00. www.ukinspain.com*

Menorca British Vice-Consulate *Sa Casa Nova, Cami de Biniatap 30, 07720 Es Castell. Tel: 971 36 33 73.*

US Embassy *Calle Serrano 75, 28006 Madrid. Tel: 91 587 22 00. Tel non-emergency citizen services: 91 587 22 40. www.embusa.es*
Australian Embassy *Plaza del Descubridor Diego de Ordas 3, 18003 Madrid. Tel: 91 353 66 00. www.spain.embassy.gov.au*

Conversion Table

FROM	TO	MULTIPLY BY
Inches	Centimetres	2.54
Feet	Metres	0.3048
Yards	Metres	0.9144
Miles	Kilometres	1.6090
Acres	Hectares	0.4047
Gallons	Litres	4.5460
Ounces	Grams	28.35
Pounds	Grams	453.6
Pounds	Kilograms	0.4536
Tons	Tonnes	1.0160

To convert back, for example from centimetres to inches, divide by the number in the third column.

Men's Suits

UK	36	38	40	42	44	46	48
Menorca & Rest of Europe	46	48	50	52	54	56	58
USA	36	38	40	42	44	46	48

Dress Sizes

UK	8	10	12	14	16	18
France	36	38	40	42	44	46
Italy	38	40	42	44	46	48
Menorca & Rest of Europe	34	36	38	40	42	44
USA	6	8	10	12	14	16

Men's Shirts

UK	14	14.5	15	15.5	16	16.5	17
Menorca & Rest of Europe	36	37	38	39/40	41	42	43
USA	14	14.5	15	15.5	16	16.5	17

Men's Shoes

UK	7	7.5	8.5	9.5	10.5	11
Menorca & Rest of Europe	41	42	43	44	45	46
USA	8	8.5	9.5	10.5	11.5	12

Women's Shoes

UK	4.5	5	5.5	6	6.5	7
Menorca & Rest of Europe	38	38	39	39	40	41
USA	6	6.5	7	7.5	8	8.5

Canadian Embassy *Núñez de Balbao 35, 28001 Madrid. Tel: 91 423 32 50. www.canada-es.org*

Republic of Ireland *Ireland House, Paseo de la Castellana 46–4, 28046 Madrid. Tel: 91 436 40 93.*

New Zealand *Plaza de la Lealtad 2,3, 28014 Madrid. Tel: 91 523 02 26.*

South Africa *Edificio Lista, Calle de Claudio Coello 91-6, Cor of j Ortega y Gasset, 28006 Madrid. Tel: 91 436 37 80.*

Emergency
The emergency number is *112*.

Health
There are no compulsory inoculations for travel to Menorca.

Medical provision is of a high standard with most staff speaking some English.

The water is potable but bottled water tastes better.

Pharmacies (*farmàcia*) sell many drugs, over the counter, however brand names vary, so if you need a specific medication/drug take an empty packet with you to aid the pharmacist or carry a prescription from your doctor.

Insurance
Having adequate health insurance cover is vital. UK citizens with a European Health Card, available from the post office, will be treated without charge but a travel insurance policy will allow repatriation if the injuries/illness warrants it. The European Health Insurance Card is available online at www.ehic.org.uk, by phoning 0845

A pharmacy

6062030 or from post offices. All other nationalities should ensure adequate cover for illness, as they will be charged at point of treatment.

Travellers should always have cover for everything they carry with them in case of loss or theft.

Insurance companies also usually provide cover for cancellation or travel delay in their policies. Though not essential this cover offers some compensation if travel plans go awry.

Lost property
You will need an official police report to make an insurance claim for any lost property. If you lose your passport, contact your Embassy or Consulate immediately.

Language
The national language of Menorca is Spanish, also know as Castilian but Menorca is part of the region of northern Spain/southern France that

PRONUNCIATION

All letters are pronounced as in English unless indicated below.

Capital	small case	Pronunciation in Catalan	Pronunciation in Castilian
C	c	Soft when followed by 'e' or 'i'. Hard at all other times	'th' before an 'e' or an 'i'
G	g	'zh' when followed by an 'e' or an 'i'. Hard at all other times.	Airy 'ch', as in 'loch' before 'e' or 'i'. Hard at all other times.
H	h	silent	silent
J	j	'j' as in the French 'Jean'	As 'ch' in loch
LL	ll	'lyuh'	'y' – Mallorca is pronounced Mayorca
N	n	Pronounced 'm' before an 'f' or an 'm'	
Ñ	ñ		'ny'. Mañana is pronounced manyana
QU	qu	Like 'k' before an 'e' or an 'i'. 'qw' before an 'a' or an 'o'.	As in the English 'k'
R	r	Rolled when it starts a word	Is always rolled
V	v		'b'
X	x		Sounds 's' before a consonant and 'ks' before a vowel
Z	z		Pronounced as a soft 'c'
IG	ig	Pronounced 'tch'	
Ç	ç	Pronounced 's'	
TX	tx	As 'ch'	
W	w		Like a 'b' or a 'v'
V	v	'b' when it starts a word but 'f' elsewhere	
X	x		'sh'

HELPFUL PHRASES

Here are a few helpful phrases

English	Catalan	Castilian
Hello	Hola	Hola
Goodbye	Adéu	Adiós
Yes	Sí	Sí
No	No	No
Do you speak English?	Parla anglès?	Habla inglés?
I don't understand	No ho entenc	No entiendo
Where is the?	On es...?	Dónde esta...?
How much is it?	Quant?	Cuanto costa?
Please	Per favor	Por favor
Thank you	Gràcies	Gracias
One	Un/una	Un/uno/una
Two	dos	dos
Three	tres	tres
Four	quatre	cuatro
Five	cinc	cinco
Six	sis	seis
Seven	set	siete
Eight	vuit	ocho
Nine	nou	nueve
Ten	deu	diez
One hundred	cent	Cien/ciento

TELÈFON D'EMERGÈNCIA **112**

GOVERN DE LES ILLES BALEARS
Conselleria de Medi Ambient
ibanat

speaks Catalan (*see pp34–5*) as the native language. Although most Menorcans speak excellent Castilian, learning a few phrases in Catalan will be appreciated. Some helpful words in both Catalan and Castilian are shown on p185.

Maps

Maó and Ciutadella tourist offices have maps of their respective towns. Basic touring maps can be picked up from the car rental companies but for a detailed map try a reputable bookstore.

Media

There are no English printed newspapers produced on Menorca but all the daily tabloids (and some broadsheets) are available at press kiosks in the major resorts and towns.

A local newspaper

ATMs can be found in major towns

Money Matters

Money

The currency of Spain (Menorca) is the euro. One euro is made up of one hundred cents. Coins come in denominations of 1, 2, 5, 10, 20 and 50 cents, 1 and 2 euros. Notes are in denominations of 5, 10, 20, 50 and 500 euros.

Currency Exchange

Almost all banks in Menorca will exchange currency and commission rates are generally low. Hotels, apartment complexes and commercial bureau de change will also exchange but will charge a higher commission fee than a bank.

Traveller's cheques

These are the safest way to carry holiday cash as they can be replaced if they are lost or stolen. You can change these at all hotels or apartment resorts, or at bureau de change and banks but the same advice applies about commission rates as with cash above.

ATMs

ATMs are becoming more numerous and you will certainly be able to get cash in the major towns. Make sure you have a Personal Identification Number (PIN) that is recognised by machines abroad. If unsure contact your bank.

Credit cards

Credit cards are widely accepted across Menorca. The most popular are MasterCard and Visa. You can also use your credit card to get cash advances over the counter in banks.

Opening hours

Shops: *generally Mon–Fri 9am–1pm & 5–8pm, Sat 9am–1pm.*
Supermarkets: *Mon–Sat 9am–8pm.*
Main Post offices: *Mon–Fri 9am–2pm & 4–7pm.* Smaller post offices: *mornings only.*
Banks: *Mon–Fri 9am–1pm.*
Museums: have varying opening hours but mainly *Tue–Sat 9am–1pm & 4–8pm.*
Pharmacies: there are duty pharmacies in all the major towns.

Police

In an emergency, call 112. There are three separate police forces in Spain:
The Guardia Civil: highways and non-urban areas. Green uniforms.
Policia Municipal: Local town police. Blue uniforms.
Policia Nacional: Riot and crowd control. Brown uniforms.

A police car in Ciutadella

Post Offices

Post offices (*correus*) can be found in all major towns and the service is reliable. Opening times are generally *Mon–Fri 9am–2pm* but offices in Maó and Ciutadella will be open in the late afternoon.

Most shops selling postcards will also sell stamps (*segells*), or head to a local tobacconist (*tabac*) and this might be an easier solution than trying to find a post office. Post boxes are a bright yellow.

Public Holidays

The following dates are official holidays in Spain – some dates are moveable so check with the tourist office. All government buildings, banks and most commercial businesses will be closed but main holiday resorts will operate as usual.

A mailbox

1 January Ano Nuevo (New Year's Day)
6 January Reyes Magos (Epiphany)
19 March Sant Josep (St Joseph's Day)
March/April Divendres Sant or Viernes Santo in Castillian (Good Friday)
1 May Dia del Trabajo (Labour Day)
Early June Corpus Christi
24 June Sant Joan's (St John's Day)
29 June Sant Pere I Sant Pau (St Peter and St Paul Day)
25 July Santiago (St James's Day)
15 August Asuncion (Assumption Day)
12 October Dia de la Hispanidad (Discovery of America Day)

1 November Todos los Santos (All Saint's Day)
6 December Dia de la Constitucion (Constitution Day)
8 December Immaculada Concepcion (Immaculate Conception)
25 December Nadal or Navidad in Castillian (Christmas Day)

Public transport
Bus

There is an excellent bus service running from Maó and linking all the major towns of the centre to Ciutadella across the spine of the island. Timetables are available at tourist offices and hotels/apartment complexes. You can buy tickets from the driver as you enter the bus.

Transports de les Illes Balears runs services across the island but 3 different companies fulfill the contracts. Transportes Menorca or TMSA (*tel: 971 38 03 93*) run services from Maó to Ciutadella, Es Castell, Punta Prima, Binibèquer, Cala'n Porter, Son Bou, Sant Tomàs and Cala de Santa Galdana.

Autocares Roca Triay (*tel: 971 15 43 90*) connects Fornells with Maó via Arenal d'en Castell, Son Parc and Es Grau.

Autocares Torres (*tel: 971 38 64 61*) connects Ciutadella with Cala'n Bosc, Cala Blanca, Cala en Blanes, Cala en Forcat and Cala Morell.

Sustainable Tourism

Thomas Cook is a strong advocate of ethical and fairly traded tourism and believes that the travel experience should be as good for the places visited as it is for the people that visit. That's why we're a firm supporter of The Travel

Excellent bus services run between major towns

Foundation: a charity that develops solutions to help improve and protect holiday destinations, their environment, traditions and culture. To find out what you can do to make a positive difference to the places you travel to and the people who live there, please visit *www.thetravelfoundation.org.uk*

Telephones

Modern hotels will usually have a direct dial phone system, but they often charge extortionate surcharges for calls. Ask about charges before you make the decision to ring home.

The country code for Menorca (Spain) is *34*. Menorcan numbers have nine digits.

Here are the main country codes should you want to make an international call from Menorca.

USA and Canada 00 1
UK 00 44
Ireland 00 353
Australia 00 61
New Zealand 00 64

Public phones are now almost 100% card (credit card or phonecard) operated. You can buy phonecards from news kiosks and tobacconists (*tabacs*). Mobile (cell) phone coverage is good in the main towns and along main highways. Check with your mobile phone company for details (cost and partner provision) of their service on Menorca.

Time

Menorca works to central European time, which is one hour ahead of Greenwich Mean Time in winter and two hours ahead in summer. If it is one o'clock in Maó it is noon in London.

Tipping

Tipping is not expected in restaurants where service is already added to the bill. If not, a 10–15 per cent tip should be added. In bars and cafés it is customary to leave small change. Always tip bellboys and room cleaners.

Toilets

Toilets are generally of a good clean standard but there are few public facilities. The best policy is to use the facilities of a café or bar, but you should buy a drink if you do.

Tourist information

There are tourist information offices on the island at the following locations:
The arrivals hall at Maó airport.
Tel: 971 15 71 15.
Moll de Llevant (in the port area), Maó.
Tel: 971 35 59 52.
Plaça de la Catedral, Ciutadella.
Tel: 971 38 26 93.
Calle de la Mer, Fornells.
Tel: 971 37 64 12.

Travellers with disabilities

Provision for travellers with mobility problems is variable. New buildings have to meet a code standard for wheelchair access and some are adapted. Always make specific enquiries with hotels if you require specially equipped rooms. By the very nature of its natural attractions, some areas will be difficult to access.

For more holiday and travel information for people with disabilities contact:
Holiday Care Services
Tel (UK): 0845 124 9971.
www.holidaycare.org.uk

ACKNOWLEDGEMENTS
Thomas Cook Publishing wishes to thank Pete Bennett, Big World Productions for the photographs in this book, and to whom the copyright in the photographs belongs.

Send your thoughts to
books@thomascook.com

We're committed to providing the very best up-to-date information in our travel guides and constantly strive to make them as useful as they can be. You can help us to improve future editions by letting us have your feedback. If you've made a wonderful discovery on your travels that we don't already feature, if you'd like to inform us about recent changes to anything that we do include, or if you simply want to let us know your thoughts about this guidebook and how we can make it even better – we'd love to hear from you.

Send us ideas, discoveries and recommendations today and then look out for your valuable input in the next edition of this title. And, as an extra 'thank you' from Thomas Cook Publishing, you'll be automatically entered into our exciting monthly prize draw.

Emails to the above address, or letters to Travellers Project Editor, Thomas Cook Publishing, PO Box 227, Unit 18, Coningsby Road, Peterborough PE3 8SB, UK.

Please don't forget to let us know which title your feedback refers to!

FOR LABURNUM TECHNOLOGIES

Design Director	Alpana Khare	**Designer**	Neeraj Aggarwal
Series Director	Sunanda Lahiri	**DTP Designer**	Manish Aggarwal
Editor	Indira Chandrashekar	**Photo Editor**	Manju Singhal

Thanks to Bikram Grewal for the index.